Function Keys for the PC

F2	Open System menu
F3	Open Options menu
F4	Open Disasters menu
F5	Open Windows menu
F10	Hide front window, switch to next window

Ctrl-Key Combinations for the PC

Ctrl-A	Auto-Bulldoze toggle
Ctrl-B	Open Budget window
Ctrl-C	Close Front window
Ctrl-E	Open Edit window
Ctrl-G	Open Graphs window
Ctrl-H	Hide front window
Ctrl-L	Load City
Ctrl-M	Open Maps window
Ctrl-P	Position current window
Ctrl-R	Resize Edit window
Ctrl-S	Save City
Ctrl-U	Open Evaluation window
Ctrl-X	Exit SimCity
Ctrl-*arrow*	Scroll Edit window

Computer users are not all alike.
Neither are SYBEX books.

We know our customers have a variety of needs. They've told us so. And because we've listened, we've developed several distinct types of books to meet the needs of each of our customers. What are you looking for in computer help?

If you're looking for the basics, try the **ABC's** series, or for a more visual approach, select **Teach Yourself**.

Mastering and **Understanding** titles offer you a step-by-step introduction, plus an in-depth examination of intermediate-level features, to use as you progress.

Our **Up & Running** series is designed for computer-literate consumers who want a no-nonsense overview of new programs. Just 20 basic lessons, and you're on your way.

SYBEX **Encyclopedias** and **Desktop References** provide a comprehensive reference and explanation of all of the commands, features and functions of the subject software.

Sometimes a subject requires a special treatment that our standard series don't provide. So you'll find we have titles like **Advanced Techniques, Handbooks, Tips & Tricks**, and others that are specifically tailored to satisfy a unique need.

You'll find SYBEX publishes a variety of books on every popular software package. Looking for computer help? Help Yourself to SYBEX.

For a complete catalog of our publications:

SYBEX Inc.
2021 Challenger Drive, Alameda, CA 94501
Tel: (510) 523-8233/(800) 227-2346 Telex: 336311
Fax: (510) 523-2373

SimCity
Strategies and Secrets

SimCity™
Strategies and Secrets

Nick Dargahi

San Francisco • Paris • Düsseldorf • Soest

Acquisitions Editor: David J. Clark
Editor: Doug Robert
Technical Editors: Dan Tauber, Lillian Chen
Word Processors: Ann Dunn, Susan Trybull
Book Designer: Elke Hermanowski
Icon Designer: Helen Bruno
Screen Graphics: Cuong Le, Delia Brown
Desktop Production Artist: Claudia Smelser
Proofreaders: Rhonda Holmes, Dina Quan
Indexer: Ted Laux
Cover Designer: Ingalls+Associates

Library of Congress Card Number: 91-75246
ISBN: 0-89588-890-4

Manufactured in the United States of America
10 9 8 7 6 5 4 3 2 1

Acknowledgments

I am greatly indebted to the many people who assisted me in the development of this book. Without their help, this project would not have been possible. Many thanks to Dr. Rudolph Langer, Dianne King, and David Clark, who gave me a chance to solo, and my editor Doug Robert, who deflated my sometimes turgid prose but always with great diplomacy. To the other staff at SYBEX, I'd like to express my thanks to Joanne Cuthbertson, who steered me in the right direction, Dan Tauber and Lillian Chen, who corrected me when I was wrong, Rhonda Holmes and Dina Quan, who proofread the book, Claudia Smelser, who desktop published the manuscript, and Delia Brown and Cuong Le, who handled the graphics. To my colleagues Michael Gross (chairman emeritus), Sharon Crawford, and Fred Horch in the Tech Department at SYBEX, I am appreciative for their good humor and spirits while I was in a frenzy trying to meet deadlines. In addition, Margaret Rowlands and Jennifer Booth both deserve mention for their contributions in designing and helping to promote the book.

Invaluable tips and strategies were provided by James Alton, A. D. Perkins—Mayor of the SimMayors Society on the Prodigy Online Service, and Eric Perlman. Their collective clues on winning the scenarios were especially helpful. Edward W. Greenberg graciously provided his shareware printing utility for SimCity which allowed me to illustrate some of the cities with great effect.

My thanks also to Will Wright, the creative genius behind SimCity, and to Steve Smythe and all the other helpful Maxis mavens. The keen insight and behind-the-scenes information they freely offered helped me to better understand the inner workings of SimCity.

Lastly, I owe everything to my family, including Xenia, Milou, Kira, and Ali, for their encouragement, understanding, and support. To Adriene goes my gratitude for being patient.

Preface

This book is intended as a companion guide to SimCity, the city simulator from Maxis. With SimCity you can design and build cities and see the results of your actions in a dynamic color graphics display (depending on your hardware and software configuration). As a system simulation, SimCity models urban design decisions and their impact on city growth. Your role in SimCity is that of Mayor, city planner, and city engineer. The zoning decisions and fiscal policies you make will determine whether your city is ultimately successful or tragically doomed.

Both the PC and Macintosh versions of SimCity are covered in this book. Where there are differences in the look and feel of the different versions of the game, they are noted and sometimes illustrated. The latest SimCity Macintosh version 1.3 is included, along with the older version 1.2 because some people may prefer to keep the version they have rather than upgrade to version 1.3. (SimCity version 1.3 for the Macintosh fixes incompatibilities with System 7 and some newer Macintoshes, but does not differ cosmetically or internally in any substantive way from version 1.2.)

The book is organized into three main parts. Part I, *An Introduction to SimCity*, is meant to introduce SimCity to novice players, leading them through the installation and then walking them through a sample game. The simulator's controls are next demonstrated along with a tutorial on how to use the various maps, menu commands, and feedback mechanisms. Part II, *SimCity Theory and Secrets*, is more for veteran SimCity players, although beginners can easily understand the sneaky tricks and tips chapter without too much travail. In this section of the book, the rules that govern the simulator are presented along with an invaluable collection of strategic secrets, tips, and tricks culled from users and electronic bulletin boards. Part III, *Winning Strategies for the Eight Model Scenarios*, is intended for beginners and advanced players alike. The eight built-in scenarios are discussed one by one, and tested strategies for winning them are presented. The appendices offer additional information on SimCity. Appendix A reveals the organization of the data structures within SimCity's city files for sophisticated players who like to tinker directly with their cities on disk. A brief overview of the ancillary programs SimCity Terrain Editor and SimCity Graphics Sets (Future Cities & Ancient Cities) is given in Appendices B and C, with accompanying illustrations.

Throughout the book you will notice special icons in the margins. The Striding stick man—our "Action" icon—indicates points where you should actually perform certain steps as you read along.

The traditional "pointing finger" notifies you of practical hints or special techniques.

The "Caution" or "Warning" symbol alerts you to potential problems.

Special "tool" icons specific to SimCity, smaller in size than those mentioned above, appear at points where the tools are first intro-duced or where you will need to identify the tools needed for important procedures. By including the tool icons in the margins we hope we have made it easy for you to skim the steps for the information you need.

If you have never played SimCity, you will find this book helpful in learning the basics of the program. If you are already familiar with SimCity, you will delight in discovering all the new sneaky tricks, tips, and secrets that make SimCity so interesting. If you have ever been frustrated by not being able to win the scenarios, you will learn how to do so. The wealth of information presented here cannot be found in any other book.

Contents at a Glance

Table of Contents

PART I

An Introduction to SimCity

Step 1

Installing Your
Version of the Program

Before you can play SimCity, you must install and configure the program to your particular computer. This step instructs you on the proper installation for both the PC and Macintosh. Hardware and system requirements for the various versions of SimCity are also discussed.

IBM PC, XT, AT, and Compatibles

The following sections describe the hardware requirements and the installation procedure for the PC version.

Hardware Requirements for Version 1.07 for the PC

SimCity version 1.07 is designed to run on any IBM, Tandy, or 100% compatible 8086/8088 or 80286/80386-based microcomputer. Although you can have as little as 512K of RAM (Random Access Memory), 640K of RAM is necessary to run high-resolution EGA/ VGA graphics. You can run SimCity with most graphics cards and monitors, including such popular graphics card standards as Hercules, Tandy, CGA, MCGA, EGA, and VGA. Of course, SimCity looks its best when run on a VGA color monitor, but you will certainly be able to play even if you have only a monochrome Hercules or EGA/VGA setup.

The program will run from a 5¼" or 3½" floppy disk or from a hard disk. For faster game execution you should install it on a hard disk, if one is available.

Note that you cannot simply insert your original SimCity disks and expect to play. The original SimCity disks can only be used to *install* SimCity on a floppy or hard disk; the program can then be run from the installed files. If you plan to run the game from a 360K 5¼" floppy disk, you must install to a blank formatted disk, and use that as your working copy. Actually, if you plan on installing SimCity to 360K 5¼" floppy disks, you will actually need to have two blank formatted disks: one for your working copy of the program, the other for holding the data you will be saving for the cities you create. Furthermore, because only the most frequently used program files will fit on your 360K working copy, in the course of play you may be asked for one of the original SimCity disks. Therefore, in addition to your working copy with the installed files and your data disk, be sure to keep your originals on hand when playing SimCity.

A mouse or joystick is highly recommended, since most of your activities in the game involve precisely positioning graphic objects on the screen.

Sound is also a feature of SimCity. You can use the built-in PC sound capability with its tinny sounding speaker or, if you are so equipped, the COVOX Sound Master board, an add-on sound card providing enhanced sound effects such as higher fidelity for digitized sound and synthesizer-generated tones for musical reproduction. If you are like most PC users, you will probably have just the built-in PC "speaker," which will give only a fair rendition of city noises.

For printing, the PC version will work only with the IBM ProPrinter or an Epson MX, RX, FX, or compatible printer hooked up to your parallel port. Unfortunately, if you have a PostScript or nonEpson-compatible laser printer—for example, any printer in the popular Hewlett-Packard LaserJet series—you are out of luck and cannot print. (The Mac version, however, works with PostScript Laser-Writers.)

There is an unauthorized shareware HP LaserJet printer program called MAP.ZIP that can be downloaded from various electronic bulletin boards. This program (discussed in Step 8) allows you to print a text-based map of any city file from the DOS prompt. Another shareware program you can try is EMUL8.EXE, which overcomes the LaserJet printer limitation by allowing any Hewlett-Packard PCL (Printer Control Language) printer to emulate an Epson FX printer. To find out where to obtain these programs, look in the CompuServe Game Forum under *Libraries* or the Prodigy game bulletin board for SimCity; if the subject is not mentioned anywhere, leave a public message and someone is sure to respond with the information on how to find it. MAP.ZIP is a compressed file and must be decompressed or unarchived using a utility called PKUNZIP, which is also a shareware program, available from most online services. The MAP.ZIP program comes with instructions.

The following is a brief summary of the hardware and system requirements for IBM PC/XT/AT or compatible microcomputers running SimCity 1.07:

- IBM, Tandy, or 100% compatible PC/XT/AT computer
- minimum 512K RAM (640K for EGA/VGA graphics)
- Hercules, Tandy, CGA, MCGA, EGA, or VGA graphics card
- color or monochrome monitor
- 1 floppy drive
- MS-DOS or PC-DOS 2.0 or greater

You can load the program more quickly and easily if you use a hard disk. The following additional peripheral devices, though optional, are recommended for their usefulness:

- Hard drive
- Mouse or analog joystick (or contact joystick if you will be using the COVOX Sound Master board)
- IBM ProPrinter or Epson MX, RX, FX, or compatible printer
- COVOX Sound Master board or Tandy Digital Sound

Future versions will support the SoundBlaster sound board (from Creative Labs).

Analog joysticks are not compatible with the COVOX Sound Master, which requires nonstandard on/off contact joysticks. The Sound Master has a port built into the card that you plug your contact joystick into. If you have another analog joystick plugged into a game port, you may have a device conflict that will result in disabling your sound capability.

Installing Version 1.07 on a Hard Disk

If you are running DOS 4.01, make sure the shell is switched off before running SimCity. Be sure *all* memory-resident software such as Norton Commander, PC Tools, and Windows are not loaded into memory. These programs take RAM space away from the area needed to run SimCity.

Verifying the Drive to Install From

Insert your original SimCity 3½" disk or Disk #1 if you only have a 5¼" drive and enter **A:INSTALL** (or **B:INSTALL** if you are using your B drive) at the DOS prompt. The installation program will immediately start up and you will be presented with the first of several option selection screens.

The first screen, as seen in Figure 1.1, prompts you for the drive you are installing from. If the asterisk correctly indicates the drive you've placed the disk into, press Enter. If not, use the left or right

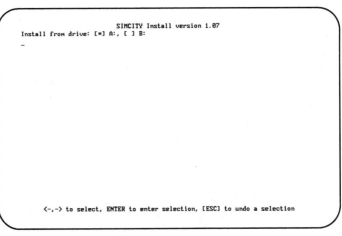

```
                         SIMCITY Install version 1.07
Install from drive: [×] A:, [ ] B:
-




                  <-,-> to select, ENTER to enter selection, [ESC] to undo a selection
```

Figure 1.1: Verifying the drive to install from

arrow key to move the asterisk into the proper drive box and then press Enter. You will next be asked to confirm if this choice is correct; type **Y** if it is correctly listed or **N** if you need to go back and change your selection.

Selecting the Drive to Install To

The next installation screen prompts you for the drive you wish to install SimCity on. Since in this section you are interested in installing to your hard disk, select **C:** or **D:**, depending on the drive you are using. The install program will ask you for the destination directory (Figure 1.2). Type in or accept the default directory destination of **C:\SIMCITY** (or **D:\SIMCITY** for the D drive). Confirm your choice when prompted by typing **Y**.

Specifying the Video Adapter

The next screen (Figure 1.3) prompts you to identify your video adapter and monitor configuration. For the VGA/EGA option, there are several subcategories for which you need to know the amount of system RAM you have, the amount of video RAM contained on your VGA/EGA card, and your monitor's resolution and display

```
                         SIMCITY Install version 1.07
           FROM drive A:

   Install to drive: [ ] A:, [ ] B:, [*] C:, [ ] D:

    Destination directory -> C:\SIMCITY
   Install TO C:\SIMCITY [n/Y]:




           <-,-> to select, ENTER to enter selection, [ESC] to undo a selection
```

Figure 1.2: Verifying the drive and directory to install to

```
                    SIMCITY Install version 1.07
        FROM drive A:
        TO C:\SIMCITY\

Display:  [ ] CGA, 640x200 b/w;              [ ] Tandy color, 320x200, 16 color;
          [ ] Hercules, 720x348 b/w
UGA/EGA: minimum Video RAM  minimum MAIN RAM  Resolution        Display Type
[x]           256k               640k         640x350 16 color   COLOR
[ ]           128k               512k         320x200 16 color   COLOR
[ ]           128k               512k         640x350 b/w        BW/COLOR
UGA/MCGA:
[ ]           N/A                512k         640x480 b/w        BW/COLOR
Install 256K EGA & 640K PC, 640x350,16 color display drivers [n/Y]:




         <-,-> to select, ENTER to enter selection, [ESC] to undo a selection
```

Figure 1.3: Selecting the video display type

type. Use the left and right arrow keys to move the cursor among the different selection options. (The up and down arrow keys will not work.) Make your selection and then type **Y** to confirm your choice.

Specifying the Joystick

In the next screen, you must indicate whether you have or plan to use a joystick. Confirm by entering a **Y** or **N**.

A word of caution is in order here. You can't have a mouse and a joystick installed at the same time. If you have a mouse driver installed on your computer, a joystick will not work. The mouse driver must be removed from your autoexec.bat or config.sys file and your machine rebooted before you can use the joystick. Also, if you have an analog (as opposed to contact) joystick and you are using the COVOX Sound Master board, you will probably experience incompatibility problems which will affect your sound.

Loading Sound Drivers

The SimCity install program will next ask you to disclose which sound options you prefer. Select from the available choices of None,

IBM, Tandy Digital, or the COVOX Sound Master, depending on which hardware you have installed in your system. Confirm by entering **Y.**

Confirming Your Choices

The next screen that pops up will recapitulate your choices for the setup and ask you to confirm them. If at any stage of the installation you make a mistake, press the Esc key to back up one step in the installation process. You can abort the installation entirely by pressing the Esc key enough times that you return to the opening installation screen, and then press the Esc key one more time to return to the DOS prompt.

After you press **Y** to accept all the installation choices, SimCity will request that your SimCity source disk be inserted in your drive to begin the file copying process. If needed, the installation program will prompt you to swap your SimCity source disk(s) in order to copy additional files. Figure 1.4 shows the installation program in the midst of copying the SimCity files to a hard disk.

After finishing, you should get a final message on screen informing you that the installation was successfully completed.

```
                         SIMCITY Install version 1.07
              FROM drive A:
              TO C:\SIMCITY\
              256K EGA & 640K PC, 640x350,16 color display
          _   No Joystick
              IBM  sound




              Reading A:SIMCITY.EXE......
              Reading A:SOUNDDAT.PSF.
              Writing C:\SIMCITY\SIMCITY.EXE......
              Writing C:\SIMCITY\SOUNDDAT.PSF.
              Looking for A:CEGANTRO.PPF
              Please insert SIMCITY source disk 2 in drive A and press ENTER



                 <-,-> to select, ENTER to enter selection, [ESC] to undo a selection
```

Figure 1.4: Installation progress report

Installing Version 1.07 on a Floppy Disk

The process for installing SimCity 1.07 to a floppy disk is much the same as it is for installing to a hard disk.

Formatting Floppy Disks

Before installing on a floppy disk, you must format two 5¼" 360K double-density disks or one 5¼" 1.2Mb high-density disk or one 3½" disk, depending on which type of disk you intend to use with your computer.

Turn on your computer, and at the DOS prompt, type **FORMAT A:** and press Enter. When prompted, insert your blank disk to be formatted. Press Enter to begin formatting.

Do not attempt to format a 360K 5¼" disk as a 1.2Mb disk, even in a high-density 1.2Mb 5¼" drive. You will not be able to read disks that you create in this format.

Begin Floppy Disk Installation

Now that you have formatted your disks, you are ready to begin the floppy disk installation. Insert your original SimCity disk and enter **A:Install** (or **B:Install** if you are using your B drive) at the DOS prompt. The installation program will start up and you will be presented with the first of several option selection screens. Go back to the hard drive installation section in this step and follow the instructions starting from the section titled *Selecting the Drive to Install To*. The only exception is that you must install SimCity in the root directory of your floppy disk (**A:** or **B:**)—do not attempt to install the program in a subdirectory on your floppy disk. The program will not run properly if you install to a subdirectory on a floppy. Otherwise, follow the steps as outlined previously for the hard disk installation.

Don't use subdirectories when installing to a floppy disk.

DOS 5.0 and Windows 3.0 for Version 1.07

Although version 1.07 is not guaranteed to be compatible with DOS 5.0 and Windows 3.0, informal testing reveals that the program seems to work well with DOS 5.0 and not so well with Windows 3.0. SimCity currently works from DOS 5.0's DOS shell, but it cannot take advantage of its task-swapping facilities, which let you jump back and forth to other applications. At the time of this writing Maxis is actively working on a Windows version of SimCity.

Macintosh Computers

The following sections detail the hardware and system requirements and installation procedures for the various Macintosh versions of SimCity.

Hardware and System Requirements

There are four Macintosh versions of SimCity. All four versions' hardware requirements will be described in this next section.

Version 1.3

SimCity's newest version, SimCity 1.3, is compatible with the new System 7 operating system from Apple and can also be run under the older System 6. Version 1.3 comes in two flavors, 1.3b&w and 1.3c.

Upgrading to Version 1.3

If you have upgraded your Macintosh to run System 7 since you originally purchased SimCity, you can obtain a free upgrade program, aproximately 180k in size, directly from Maxis. You can also obtain the upgrade via CompuServe and other electronic BBS (Bulletin Board System) services. Note that if you use the upgrade program, your present SimCity program will be modified strictly according to whether it is the color or b&w version. This means that if you have SimCity 1.2b&w, then the upgrade program will transform it into version 1.3b&w and will only run in black and white.

(Version 1.3b&w will run on a color system if you set the monitor control panel to black and white.) Similarly, if you have SimCity 1.2c, the upgrade program will change it into version 1.3c, which runs SimCity in color. Copy protection remains for 1.3b&w; 1.3c has no copy protection.

Table 1.1 lists the various compatiblity issues for all the different Macintosh versions.

Why Upgrade to SimCity 1.3?

You only need version 1.3 if you are running SimCity under Macintosh System 7 or if you are having compatibility problems with your computer. Otherwise, you are better off with version 1.2. In fact, unless you are using System 7, version 1.2c is faster than version 1.3c.

For users who have version 1.3 but would rather run 1.2, Maxis offers a "downgrade" to version 1.2.

Version 1.2c

SimCity Deluxe, also known as SimCity Color Mac II Version 1.2c, is not fully compatible with System 7.0. If you want to run under System 7, you must upgrade to version 1.3. A free update program from Maxis is available which will modify any current version of SimCity you now have and make it a System 7 compliant version 1.3c (see *Upgrading to Version 1.3* in this step). With System 6.0.7, you must run under the MultiFinder.

You must have at least 2 Mb of RAM and a monitor capable of displaying either 16 colors or 16 gray scales in order to run this version of the program. SimCity only displays 16 colors at a time, so you must set the monitor control panel to 16 colors before you can play the game. SimCity 1.2c will not run on the internal monitor that is built into the SE/30. As a result, if you wish to use the SE/30, you must have an external color or gray scale monitor set up.

Model or CPU

	1.2b&w	1.2c	1.3b&w	1.3c
512e	✓		✓ [7]	
Plus	✓ [1]		✓	
SE	✓ [1]		✓	
SE/30	✓ [1,5]	✓ [2,3]	✓ [5]	✓ [2,3,4]
Classic	✓ [1]		✓ [4]	
LC		✓ [1,2]	✓ [5]	✓ [2,4]
II	✓ [1,5]	✓ [2]	✓ [5]	✓ [2,4]
IIx	✓ [1,5]	✓ [2]	✓ [5]	✓ [2,4]
IIcx		✓ [1,2]	✓ [5]	✓ [2,4]
IIsi		✓ [1,2]	✓ [5]	✓ [2,4]
IIci		✓ [1,2]	✓ [5]	✓ [2,4]
IIfx		✓ [1,2]	✓ [5]	✓ [2,4]

Operating System

	1.2b&w	1.2c	1.3b&w	1.3c
System 6	✓	✓	✓	✓ [4]
System 7		✓ [6]	✓	✓

Notes

1. System 6 only (or System 6.0.7 with Multifinder).

2. Color or gray-scale monitor.

3. Not compatible with internal monitor built into SE/30.

4. On machines running System 6, version 1.3 is slower than version 1.2. You may want to downgrade your copy of SimCity to version 1.2.

5. On color systems, monitor control panel must be set to black and white.

6. Mac II or IIx only.

7. 1 Mb of RAM required.

Table 1.1: Macintosh/SimCity Compatibility and Issues

Aside from the gorgeous color graphics that this version has to offer, you will appreciate the fact that 1.2c has no copy protection. This means that you can start a game without having to consult the pernicious copy-protection sheet (discussed later in this step).

Version 1.2b&w

SimCity version 1.2b&w will not work reliably with System 7. If you intend to run under System 7, you must upgrade your version 1.2b&w to 1.3b&w using a free update program (see *Upgrading to Version 1.3* in this step).

Although previous Systems will work with SimCity, System 6.0.7 will only work under MultiFinder, which you will need to set under the Mac's **Special/Setup** menu if it is not already running. Remember that if you select the MultiFinder, your change will not take effect until you restart your machine using the **Special/Shutdown** or **Special/Reset** menu command.

When using the program with the Mac 512e, you need to run a much earlier version of the Mac operating system than System 6. This is because the ROM chips in the early Macintoshes are not compatible with the system software that was developed for the Mac Plus and succeeding Macintosh models. And, although not recommended, you can run SimCity 1.2b&w on a Mac 512 with 400K drives. See the installation section for precise instructions. When running version 1.2 all the Macintoshes that can use color must have the monitor control panel set to black and white.

Installation

The following sections tell you how to install each Macintosh version of SimCity.

Installing Version 1.3

There are two ways to install SimCity version 1.3 to your computer. You can buy a complete SimCity 1.3 disk and copy it along with its accompanying scenario file to your hard disk or you can order the upgrade program for 1.3 that will upgrade any version of SimCity for the Macintosh and turn it into version 1.3. There is not enough room for the scenario file on the color version (1.3c) floppy disk, so you cannot run 1.3c from floppy; you must run it on a hard drive. Use the scenario file that came with your old b&w or color version of SimCity and copy it into the same folder on your hard disk that you put SimCity 1.3. To install onto your hard disk, simply create a new folder on the hard disk, give it a name such as **SimCity Folder**, and then drag the SimCity icon and the Scenario file into the folder.

Installing Version 1.2c

Because there is no room for the scenario file on the Color Mac II version 1.2c floppy disk, you cannot run the SimCity scenarios from a floppy disk; the only way to properly use SimCity 1.2c is to install it on a hard drive. Just use the scenario file that came with your old b&w or color version of SimCity and copy it into the same folder on your hard disk that you put SimCity 1.2c. To do this, simply create a new folder on the hard disk, give it a name such as **SimCity Folder**, and then drag the SimCity icon and the Scenario file into the folder.

Installing Version 1.2b&w

There is no installation procedure for SimCity if you are running it from a floppy (except the Mac 512 400K disk version—see below). Just make sure that the SimCity program icon is on the same disk as the scenario file icon. If you are installing to a hard disk, simply create a new folder on your hard disk, give it a name such as **SimCity Folder**, and then drag the SimCity icon and the Scenario file into the folder.

Installing to a Mac 512 with 400K Drives

The instructions for installing SimCity to an older Mac 512 with 400K drives is a little bit involved, but once it's done you can forget about it. First transfer the SimCity program from your 800K original disk to a blank 400K formatted floppy disk by using a Mac 512e or later that can use both 400K and 800K disks. The black and white

SimCity program takes up only 362K of disk space, so you will have no problem transferring it to a blank 400K disk. You will not, however, be able to install a System and Finder file on the same disk, due to space limitations; therefore you must play SimCity using a dual drive system with one disk containing your "boot" disk and the other the SimCity program. After booting up from your floppy disk that has a system that works with the Mac 512, insert your 400K SimCity program disk that you just created and then run SimCity from the 400K floppy.

Copy Protection

The PC and Macintosh 1.2b&w and 1.3b&w versions of the game are copy protected. There is no copy protection for Macintosh versions 1.3c and 1.2c.

The issue of copy protection has been addressed in a fairly innocuous way so that you may back up your disks without restrictions. Maxis has chosen a non-disk-based copy protection scheme involving tables that you must consult each time you start up the game. The table itself is printed on a red sheet of paper that makes photocopying impossible, and contains shaded box symbols that refer to various cities and their respective populations around the world. At the beginning of a game session, the SimCity program will pop up a dialog box that will display a random combination of the shaded box symbols along with a query as to which city or population the symbols refer to.

Step 2

Playing SimCity

In this step, you will be introduced to SimCity. You will learn why it is called a "system simulation," and you will learn what it attempts to simulate. You will then be quickly immersed in a sample game. Common keyboard and mouse selection techniques will be described, along with a brief presentation of the Maps and Edit windows. During your initial foray as "Mayor" of SimCity, you will be presented with some basic concepts that will aid you in designing future cities.

What Is SimCity?

SimCity is a new type of entertainment/educational software categorized not as a game but as a *system simulation,* a program that attempts to represent or reproduce "real-world" conditions and phenomena under the governance of strict rules or laws. The simulator is a tool that enables users to model, under test conditions, phenomena that would likely occur in actual life. By identifying and observing elementary processes and how they interact, programmers have been able to simulate very complex systems.

As computing power increases year by year, so does the complexity and sophistication of simulation software. With the advent of 32-bit microprocessors for personal computers (starting at the 80386 level), vastly improved simulations are bringing personal computer users closer than ever to mimicking the real world. Simulations exist of aircraft, submarines, ships, and automobiles as well as of political, military, and ecological systems.

By creating an artificial model of urban city life, the SimCity simulation demonstrates the potentially successful or disastrous consequences of city planning decisions. The system model is extremely complex, governed by over a hundred rules, and is regulated by many variables, which can be controlled by the player. Because there is no opponent, SimCity offers a noncompetitive environment in which to explore, experiment, and create new types of cities. You can make your own goals by designing your own city, or you can attempt to master the eight built-in scenarios, tackling specific urban problems such as crime, unemployment, pollution, traffic, fire, floods, and earthquakes, and in so doing gain insight into the processes that make a city manageable or intractable. There is no one way to win or succeed with SimCity, so you need not fear that you will be bored soon because you have discovered how to "beat the machine." Random elements, such as disasters or other "acts of God," introduce uncertainties into the game, so you can never expect that your city will be completely safe. Starting from scratch, you can watch the village you've designed evolve into a megalopolis, all the while fine-tuning the process of growth. Or, using a pre-existing city model, you can attempt to rectify intransigent problems before they become insurmountable and you, as mayor of SimCity, are turned out of office.

Starting a New City

First, boot up your computer and start SimCity. With a PC you must first change your current drive or directory so that you are in the directory that contains the SimCity files. For example, if SimCity is on your C drive in a directory called SIMCITY, you would type **C:** then **cd\Simcity** and then **SIMCITY** to begin the game. If you installed SimCity on a floppy disk, put the disk in the drive and type in the drive identifier (**A:** or **B:**), and then type **SIMCITY**. For Macintosh users, just double-click the mouse pointer on the SimCity icon to initiate the program.

The initial SimCity screen looks like Figure 2.1. You should see a pointer icon resembling a hand somewhere on or near the road sign.

Selection Techniques

In the course of this book I will use terms such as *select, point, click on, double-click,* or *click and drag* with regard to the pointer or cursor icon on your screen. On the PC the SimCity pointer appears as a hand; on the Macintosh it looks like a typical mouse pointer, that is, a diagonally pointing arrow. The pointer is controlled by the mouse, keyboard, or joystick.

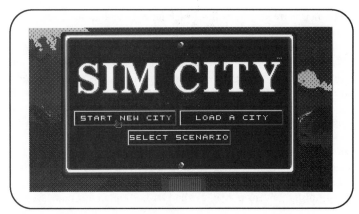

Figure 2.1: The SimCity road sign

Select will mean to position the pointer on a screen object and then click or press the left or main mouse button, the joystick button, or the space bar. **Point** will mean to position the pointer using the mouse, joystick, or cursor keys. **Click on** and **double-click** are essentially synonymous with **select,** except that double-clicking involves pressing the mouse button twice in quick succession. **Click and drag** refers to the process of selecting something and then moving the pointer to another position, all the while holding down the mouse button, the joystick button, or the space bar.

For those who will be using only the keyboard in the PC version of SimCity, the gray + and – keys on the numeric keypad section of your keyboard will cycle through and highlight the different icon tools that allow you to control the simulator. Once a tool or other item is highlighted, press Enter or the space bar to initiate the corresponding action.

For keyboard users

On every version of SimCity, you will have the following choices:

- **Start New City**
- **Load A City**
- **Select Scenario**

Let's begin by selecting the **Start New City** button. The screen shown in Figure 2.2 will appear, allowing you to choose a name for your city and a difficulty level. For now, accept the default name of "Heresville" (on the Mac the new city is called "SomeWhere") and select the **Easy** game play level, then select **OK**. The different difficulty levels control the amount of money you start off with in the city treasury ($20,000, $10,000, or $5,000), as well as how prone you are to disasters and how mild-tempered your SimCitizens are.

SimCity will next start "terraforming" your new city, creating a new landform on which to base your dream city. If you're a Macintosh user you will have the option of re-terraforming if your terrain is unappealing; but for now click the **OK** button to continue.

Copy Protection

At this point, except for the color Macintosh versions (1.2c and 1.3c) in which there is no copy protection, SimCity will ask you for the name or population of a city that is on the red sheet entitled *SimCity All-Time High Scores*. This four-part chart is included with your software package and is colored red to make it impossible to duplicate on a copy machine, effectively limiting the use of it to the person who legitimately bought the program. Without the information on the sheet you cannot play the game.

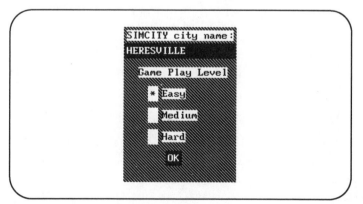

Figure 2.2: Selecting the difficulty level

The copy protection works by having you match three randomly selected box symbols displayed on the screen (as in Figure 2.3) with box symbols on the table. You must first find the page that shows the first box in its upper right corner; on that page you must find the second and third boxes as a pair. On the line to the immediate right of the box symbols you will find the city or population to be entered in the copy protection text box. You are given three chances to type the correct information; if you blow it completely you must re-start the game from scratch. Go ahead and look up the symbols now, and enter the proper population or city depending on the message.

If you have passed through the copy protection gauntlet, a message will pop up on the screen congratulating you. If you fail all three attempts to pass the copy protection feature of SimCity, you will be presented with a message warning you that the CopyProtect test failed and to beware of the city's wrath. Should you ignore this warning and continue to play, disasters will strike your city faster than you can make any progress.

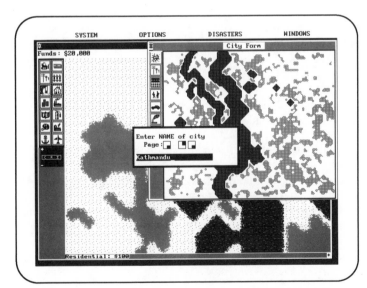

Figure 2.3: The copy protection box with answer from the red sheet

The Map and Edit Windows

You will be alternating between two overlapping windows to build your city and gather information. The Maps window, initially called the City Form window (on the Macintosh it is initially called City Map:Comprehensive) and the Edit window are used in conjunction with the various tool or symbol icons that appear in a palette to the left of each window. The Maps window, initially on the right of your screen, shows you a complete view of your city environs, offering you various display options that portray such factors as crime rates, pollution, land value, population, traffic density, city services, the power grid, and transportation links. The Edit window, initially on the left of the screen, displays an enlargement of the portion of the Maps window that you have currently selected (the moveable rectangle that you can click and drag in the Maps window).

All the main simulation controls are to be found in the Edit window, so it is in this window that you actually make decisions about zoning and the construction of your city's infrastructure.

The active window

You can select or use items in only one window at a time, but you can easily switch from that window to another to carry out your actions. The window that is currently active is the one that overlaps. In Figure 2.4, the active window is the "City Form" Maps window. The active window on the PC shows a highlighted border; on the Macintosh it is indicated by striped horizontal grooves in the top or "title" bar of the window.

To jump to the other open window, just position the pointer in the window you wish to make active and select it or press Enter. The Macintosh's Maps window offers a shortcut method of switching to the Edit window: simply double-click on the selection rectangle. In later steps, you will learn about other efficient methods of moving around on your map. Select the Edit window now, thereby making it the active window, and notice how its appearance changes. Then jump back to the other window before continuing.

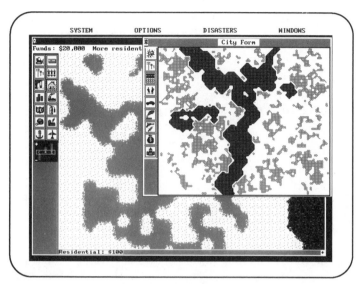

Figure 2.4: The active "City Form" Maps window overlapping the Edit window

Navigating the Maps Window

At present, your "City Form" Maps window should be active and you should be able to move the transparent selection rectangle by clicking and dragging it with the mouse or joystick or the keyboard cursor keys. Keyboard users need to hold down the space bar while pressing the cursor-movement keys in order to select and drag the rectangle pointer. Try this now as a simple exercise, then switch to the Edit window to make it active.

Navigating the Edit Window

When you need to scroll the Edit window to display something that is off screen, the Macintosh version gives you scroll boxes and scroll bars imbedded in the window's edges in addition to a "joystick box" in the upper right corner of the screen.

Note that scrolling does not actually move the Edit window itself—it just moves more contents into view from the edge or corner you have selected.

You use the joystick box by clicking and holding the pointer on any one of the box's edge or corner squares to scroll the Edit window in a corresponding direction. For example, clicking the square on the box's bottom right corner will have the effect of scrolling the Edit window diagonally down to the right, and clicking on the upper middle square will have the effect of scrolling it up.

The PC version offers a simpler method of scrolling. Just move your pointer off the edge of your screen in the direction you wish to move. When you have scrolled as much as you need, move the pointer back onto the Edit window and scrolling will stop.

Of course, in both PC and Macintosh versions, you can return to the Maps window and reposition the selection rectangle (which shows the currently visible portion of the Edit window) and then jump back to the Edit window. The advantage of this method is that you can position the contents of the Edit window more quickly relative to the entire map.

Designing Your First City

To build a city, you must zone different areas for living, working, and shopping. In order for a city to develop, you must plan and build a transportation network enabling the Sims to travel to and from their places of business, and utility lines for supplying electricity from power plants to each residential, commercial, and industrial zone. Without this infrastructure in place, industry will die, commerce will wither, and the Sims will vote with their feet by moving out of town. Everything you do costs your taxpayers money, so if you go on a building or zoning spree, you may soon find that you have run out of funds. Also, remember that all roads, bridges, rail transit, tunnels, police stations, and fire stations have yearly maintenance costs that must be paid out of the General Fund each year.

Chronologically, the simulator advances month by month, and every January a new budget is requested in which you can decide spending priorities and set the tax rate. Setting the tax rate above 8 percent causes growth to slow and Sims to emigrate, while reducing funding for city services causes the city to unravel, with crime, fires, and transportation disruptions. In previous versions of SimCity you could get away with an ingenious trick known as the Banzai tax, whereby you raise taxes in December, collect them in January, and then lower them again immediately—with the net result being as if you had collected at the higher tax rate all year long, but were being judged well for low tax policies. In the present version of the game you can use the Banzai method once, but the Sims will complain vehemently the next time you raise taxes late in the year. If you're an unscrupulous politician, you must find other ways to fleece the public.

You might think that reducing or eliminating the tax altogether might not be a bad idea to encourage growth and immigration, but there is a price to be paid. Someone has to pay the piper, and since SimCity does not allow deficit spending, you must spend money out of your budget reserves, thus having a negative cash flow. It is important to strike a balance, such that you don't overspend or overtax, yet still maintain a stable environment for the Sims to live in.

SimCity does not allow deficit spending

Prepare now to assume the mantle of mayor, urban designer, city planner, and tax collector.

Place Residential Zones

With the Maps window currently active, move the selection rectangle to an empty land area, preferably near a river or waterfront. What you can see of the Edit window should immediately show you an enlarged view of the land area you have just selected, as in Figure 2.5.

You will want to first try zoning residential areas close to water, parks, forests, and the area you consider "downtown," because

SimCity considers these areas to be the most desirable, and thus more valuable. Switch now to the Edit window; it should overlap the Maps window. At this point you are ready to select the Residential Zone icon from the icon palette on the far left hand side of the window. Select the Residential Zone icon by clicking on it with the mouse, joystick, or keyboard (keyboard users select using the space bar). Figure 2.6 shows the pointer selecting the proper icon, which resembles a house with a small chimney on the right-hand side.

Next, move the pointer back to the central part of the Edit window. Your pointer should transform itself into an outline of a large square. This outline tells you how much clear space the residential zone will require on the map. Choose a suitable location to place your first zone, and then click on it. You should see a new residential zone in the Edit window along with an "R" indicating that it is a residential zone, and a flashing thunderbolt or lightning symbol in the center. The flashing lightning symbol tells you that the zone is not powered, and needs to be connected to a power line supplying electricity.

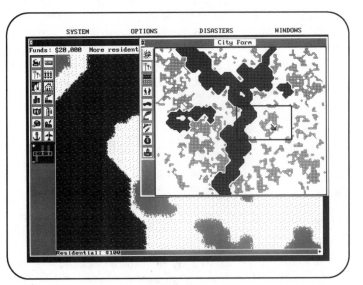

Figure 2.5: Selecting a suitable place to build your city

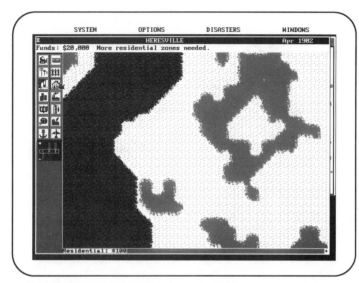

Figure 2.6: Selecting the Residential Zone icon

Without power, Sims will not move in and stay in your newly developed zone. Note that you cannot zone residences on water or over other zones. It is possible, however, to overlap residential zones to increase housing density using a technique that will be described in a later step. For now, place three more residential zones in a row so that their sides are touching. Figure 2.7 demonstrates one such arrangement.

Construct a Power Plant

Since you need to generate electricity for the development of SimCity, you will need to build a power plant. The Power Plant icon is located three icons down from the house icon on the icon palette, and looks like a factory with a lightning bolt striking it. Follow the same general procedure in selecting the Power Plant icon, but this time when clicking on it you will be presented with a small submenu that gives you the option of constructing a coal or nuclear power plant. Use the cursor keys or the mouse pointer to choose the coal-fired plant and then click to complete your entry. As before, an

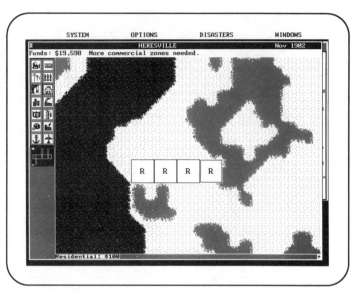

Figure 2.7: Placing unpowered residential zones

outline of a square will appear on the Edit window, telling you how much empty land area the desired zone requires. Move this square to a location suitably far away from the residential zones you have just built and then click to build your power plant. A large building with smokestacks belching ugly soot should appear.

Connect Power Lines between
Residential Zones and Power Plant

To get development in your zone going, you need to build power lines to conduct the electricity needed between the power plant and residential zones. Click the Power Line icon, located directly below the Bulldozer icon, and your pointer should become a small square when you move it back to the map in the Edit window. Place the pointer adjacent to the residential zone that is closest to the power plant and click to build your first segment of power line. By clicking and dragging, you can build enough segments to link your residential zone to your power plant. Make sure that there are no breaks or interruptions in the line. If you make a mistake, you can use the Bulldozer (see below) to knock down the wayward section. If you are successful, your residential zones will stop flashing the lightning symbol, indicating that power is being supplied to all the zones, as shown in Figure 2.8. In a few moments, Sims will start building homes, which you will see by the presence of small houses cropping up in various parts of the zones.

Any zone that borders another zone already hooked up to the power line network is considered electrically connected. Since the zones you have built so far should all be touching each other, you need only build one power line for them all to be connected.

Bulldoze Your Problems Away

The bulldozer functions like an eraser in SimCity. It serves to delete mistakes you may have made in laying out roads or power lines, demolishes eyesores that you have allowed to develop, creates landfill along waterways, clears trees and parks, and wipes out any

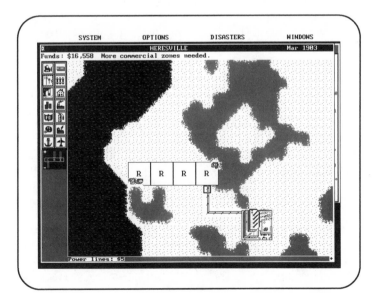

Figure 2.8: The power plant connected to your residential zones

zone that you have established. You simply select the icon that resembles a bulldozer and click on the item in the Edit window map that you wish to remove or fill in with clear land. If you wish to remove a zone, position the Bulldozer square over the center of the zone and click.

With the PC version the right mouse button will enable the Bulldozer function even if you have selected another tool. Simply press and hold down the right mouse button to bring up the bulldozer's small selection square. Try bulldozing some roads and then rebuilding them. With residential zones, you have the additional capability of bulldozing just the sides of the zone, leaving the center intact. This is useful for situations where you don't have enough room to place a needed road or transit line and for placing overlapping zones to create higher density districts.

Establish an Industrial Zone

Your next responsibility to your constituents is to provide employment prospects by establishing industrial zones for them to work in. Industrial zones are primarily useful in the early part of the game in developing an export-based economy that is strongly dependent on external markets. The local economy may thus rise and decline due to external conditions that you have no control over. Select the Industrial Zone icon (directly below the Residential Zone icon) and, once you have decided on an appropriate location, place an industrial zone near your residential zones by clicking on the large square outline. You should see a square zone with the letter "I" in the center denoting that it is an Industrial zone, along with a flashing lightning symbol telling you that the zone is unpowered. Build three more industrial zones, all sharing sides in a block formation, and then connect them to the power grid using the methods previously outlined. When the zones are properly powered up, the Sims will start to build factories and light industry, which you will see by the activity in the zones. SimCity is a dynamic game, with many changes occurring as time progresses, so if industry disappears from the zone from time to time it is because various factors have discouraged development or caused businesses to fold and move out of town.

Zone Commercial Districts

In order for commerce to develop, you must plan commercial districts where the Sims can shop and transact business. In later stages of the game, commercial zones assume greater importance in the development of a robust internal economy. Select the Commercial Zone icon, located to the immediate left of the Industrial Zone icon, and move the pointer back into the map portion of the Edit window. The pointer will become a large square outline that, as before, indicates how much clear land is necessary to create the intended zone. Click to establish your first zone as close as you can to your residential zones without touching. Next, set up three more commercial zones, sharing sides, in a row adjacent to the first, so that you can hook them all up with a single power line. Then select the Power Line icon and connect the nearest commercial zone to the nearest residential zone.

Build Roads to Link Your Zones

The Sims will now be clamoring for more roads, so that they may get to work and do their shopping. Your next task is to build roads between your residential, commercial and industrial Zones, creating a transportation link that will enable your city to grow. The Road icon, the top right tool on the tool (icon) palette, allows you to build roads and bridges. Click the Road icon and it should become a small square when you move the pointer over the land in the Edit window. Roads are constructed as with the Power Line tool, by clicking on the square pointer, or by clicking and dragging. Start building your roads now, and try to connect all your zones so that the Sims can travel between zones. Very soon thereafter, you will see traffic crowding the streets, especially at curves and intersections.

Figure 2.9 illustrates how your city might look after a few years.

Understanding Funds and Budgeting

At the top of your Edit window is the *title bar,* which includes such information as your city name and the current month and year. Below the title bar is the *message bar.* From time to time messages

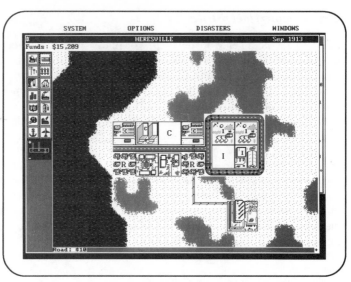

Figure 2.9: Commercial and industrial zones connected to a power grid and serviced by roads

will pop up here telling you that the Sims need something or that some disaster has been reported. On the far left side of the message bar you will see the total amount of funds remaining in your city treasury. In the box near the bottom left corner of the Edit window, you will see a description of the currently selected tool icon, and its associated cost per use.

Call up the Budget window (shown in Figure 2.10) by selecting the Windows menu and clicking on the **Budget** command. At the top of this window you can set the Tax Rate (the property tax rate) from a minimum of 0 percent to a maximum of 20 percent by clicking the up or down arrows. For now click the up arrow next to the Tax Rate percentage indicator, to raise property taxes to 8 percent. In addition, you can set funding levels for Transportation, the Police Department, and the Fire Department by clicking the up or down arrows to set the percentage you wish to allocate (as compared to the amount each department requested). Accept the funding levels as they are for now, but notice the amount of taxes you are taking in as well as the cash flow.

Cash Flow represents the difference between the taxes you collect
and the expenditures you allocate for the Police, Fire, and Transportation departments. Negative cash flows are deleterious to your
pocketbook and are shown bracketed in parentheses. When you are
finished agonizing over these budget figures, click the **Go with
these figures** button at the bottom of the window to return to the
simulator. If you dawdle too long, however, SimCity will exit the
Budget window automatically, assuming that you are being inatten-
tive, or derelict in your duties.

The Demand Indicators

Below the icon palette in the Edit window is the Demand indicator.
This bar chart displaying the relative needs for new Commercial
(C), Residential (R), and Industrial (I) zones is useful in guiding
your decisions on zoning. The plus and minus levels of the chart
indicate the relative need or lack of need for each type of zone.

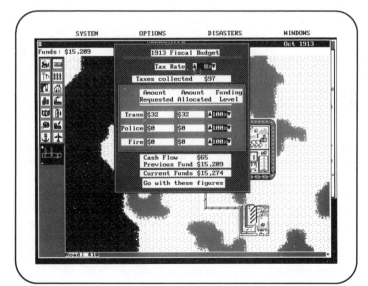

Figure 2.10: The Budget window

Evaluating Your Performance

As Mayor of SimCity, you might wish to obtain some feedback on your performance by the SimCitizens. The Sims are quite vocal about their likes and dislikes, so you must be attentive to their needs and must not ignore the opinion polls. The public opinion polls and a census count, along with other important statistics, are displayed in the Evaluation window (Figure 2.11), which you can access through the Windows menu. Call up the Evaluation window now by clicking on the Windows menu and then clicking on the **Evaluation** option.

Notice the opinion poll figures on your popularity ("Is the mayor doing a good job?"), and the citizenry's main complaints ("What are the worst problems?"). Glance also at the Net Migration and current Population statistics to learn how much your city is growing or declining. When you are finished, exit the Evaluation window—on the PC, by clicking the pointer anywhere in the window, or on the Macintosh, by clicking in the close box at the upper right corner of the window.

Saving Your City for Later Play

Because you will frequently want to replay cities that you have created, you should understand how to use the Save feature of SimCity. Let's try saving the city that you have just created. Pull down SimCity's System menu (PC version) or File menu (Macintosh version) and select the **Save** command. On the PC, you will see a dialog box with a **Save** button and text field at the top. On the Macintosh, you will see a dialog box with a text field at the bottom and a **Save** button on the right hand side. For now, accept the default name—**Heresvil.cty** or **SomeWhere**—by simply clicking the **Save** button. The dialog box will disappear, letting you know that your city was saved in a disk file. When you have completed this task, you can exit the SimCity program by pulling down the System or File menu again and selecting **Exit** or **Quit**.

You may either exit the program now or continue on to the next step, keeping the current game open.

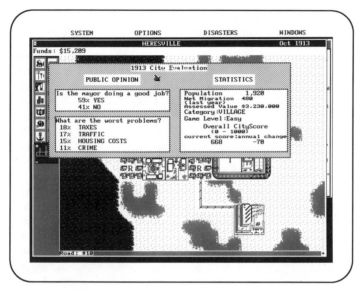

Figure 2.11: The Evaluation window

Summary

You have now learned the basics of controlling SimCity and building your own city from the ground up. In further steps, we will go into more detail about these and other features of SimCity, including the built-in scenarios.

Step 3

Founding Your City

In this step you will learn basic file commands for getting your city started. You will also learn how to save your city with different names at different times so that you may return to specific points in the city's development in order to test alternative approaches to dealing with its problems.

Although their menu names differ, the Macintosh and PC versions of SimCity have functionally equivalent pull-down menus. Both the **System** menu on the PC and the **File** menu on the Mac allow you to start new cities, load cities, save cities, load scenarios, and exit the program. (The print option will be discussed in Step 8.) This step will begin with the PC's System menu and will conclude with the Macintosh's File menu. You may skip over whichever section does not apply to your system.

In both versions you will find keyboard equivalents for some (not all) of the menu commands, as shown in Figure 3.1. These key combinations enable you to activate certain menu options from the keyboard rather than from the pull-down menu if you wish.

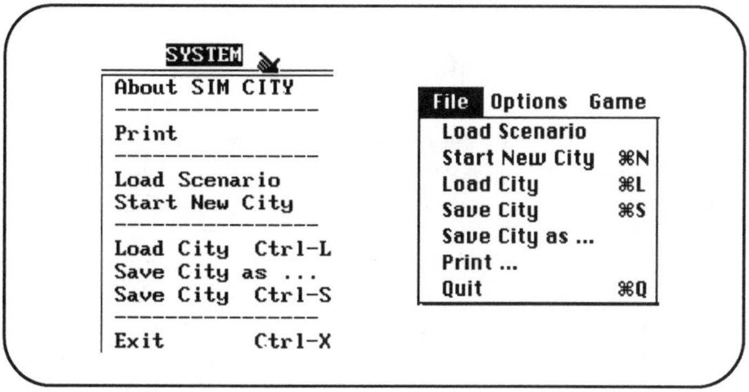

Figure 3.1: The System menu (PC) and the equivalent File menu (Macintosh)

Using the System Menu on the PC

To pull down the System menu (in order to view the various options that are available), use your mouse to move the pointer onto the menu name and click once. Alternatively, you can hold down the Alt key and press the first letter of the menu name, in this case the *S* key on your keyboard. This is the general technique for using the keyboard to pull down a menu. In the case of the System menu, you also have a second keyboard alternative: press the F2 function key. Immediately, the menu should pop open, giving you eight commands to choose from.

How to
select
menu
options

You will make your selection by clicking once on the command you wish to use, or, using the keyboard, pressing the up or down arrow keys or the first letter of the menu option to highlight the choice and then pressing Enter. For menu options that begin with the same letter, pressing the letter key repeatedly will cycle you through all the commands that begin with that letter. For example, pressing the *S* key several times while the System menu is open will cause you to highlight the **Start New City** option, then the **Save City as** option, and then the **Save City** option before returning to the **Start New City** command. While the pull-down menu is open, you may at any time close the menu without choosing an option by clicking the pointer anywhere outside the menu box, or by pressing the Esc key.

Creating Your New City

If you are continuing your game from the last step, keep SimCity open and skip to the next paragraph. Otherwise, start up SimCity so that the road sign screen appears and then click on the **Start a New City** button. You will be asked to enter the name of your city and set the game play level. For now, accept the defaults and click **OK**. Once the terrain map is terraformed you will be asked the copy protection question (see Step 2). Passing the copy protection challenge allows you to view the Edit and Maps windows.

Now pull down the System menu and select **Start New City**. This command starts you off with empty terrain on which you can build your city. If you are already in the midst of another city game, you will first be asked if you are sure you want to begin a different one: "New Game—Are You Sure?" Answering Yes will erase the city that is currently loaded. Answering No will continue your present city, giving you a chance to save it if you want. For now, let's create a new city by answering **Yes**.

Next, you will be permitted to set the game play level to Easy, Medium, or Hard and to give a new name to your city. Essentially, the game play level of **Easy** starts you off with $20,000, the **Medium** level allows you $10,000, and the **Hard** level grants you a measly $5,000. At the Hard level, it is very difficult to meet the demands of a growing city and appease the Sims at the same time. The Easy level gives you more latitude and freedom to plan your city without worrying too much about lack of money. Even at the Easy level, though, you must watch your expenditures and not overspend.

Giving Your City a Name

If it does not already appear in the City Name box, type in the name **Heresville** to give your city its new name. Press Enter to complete your entry, then choose **Easy** for the game play level, as shown in Figure 3.2. When you are finished, click the **OK** button to terraform your new city.

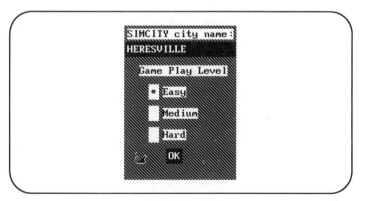

Figure 3.2: The Box for entering the city name and choosing the game play level

Saving Your City for Later Play

At some point you will probably want to freeze a game at a certain stage in its development so that you may return to it at a later time and start where you left off. If you are simply planning on exiting SimCity in order to get something else accomplished in your life, you need only select the **Save City** option from the System menu before exiting the program. If you want to save the game at a certain stage mainly so you can come back to it after playing through that stage—in order to compare the results of different approaches, for example—you should save the problem stage and the resulting outcome *as different files*. In order to do this, you need to use the **Save City as...** option instead of the **Save City** option.

In fact, you may find that you want to save the game at numerous points in order to try alternative approaches to a number of problems. Whenever you are interested in saving various stages or versions of the same game, be sure to use **Save City as** and to give each version a different name.

Using the Save City Option

The **Save City** option saves a scenario or city to disk. (Keyboard aficionados can use the *Ctrl-S* keyboard equivalent to invoke this option.) If the game in progress has the same name as a city previously saved to the same directory, SimCity will prompt you for an acknowledgement before it overwrites the previous disk file name.

The first time you choose **Save City** when playing a new city or scenario—one that hasn't been saved before—SimCity will display a dialog box to enable you to name the city as your own should you wish to do so. This is the same dialog box that appears when you choose the **Save City as** option, which is discussed below. At all other times, choosing **Save City** merely asks you to confirm whether it should overwrite the previously saved version of the city.

Using the Save City As Option

When you select the **Save City as** option from the System menu, the Save City dialog box (Figure 3.3) will pop up on the screen for you to decide what name to give your city and where to store the file.

Looking at Figure 3.3, you will see a text box, **Save** and **Cancel** buttons, and a file list box with scroll bar that displays the files and/ or subdirectories in the destination directory. Just above the list box is the name of the currently selected destination drive and directory. Moving up to a parent directory is accomplished by clicking on the double dot symbol (..) inside the list box. Descending to a file or subdirectory is accomplished by clicking on the appropriate name within the list. Clicking on the scroll bar's up and down arrows moves the files list up or down accordingly. The drive selectors indicated by the bracketed letters **[A]**, **[B]**, **[C]**, etc., allow you to to choose a different drive. Simply click on the one you want.

For keyboard users, the + and – keys on the numeric keypad move you sequentially among the various elements of the dialog box, and the space bar selects the item you want.

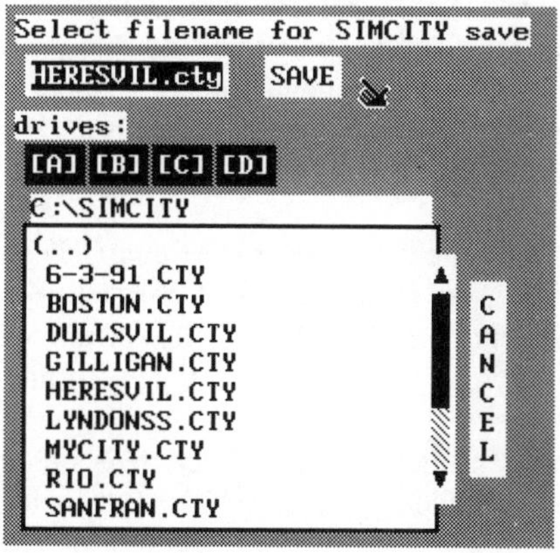

*For key-
board
users*

Figure 3.3: The Save City dialog box

Make sure that you are in the directory where you keep your SimCity files and then type in **MYCITY** in the text box next to the **Save** button. Press Enter, then click on the **Save** button to save your city to disk. If a city file with the same name already exists on your disk, you will be asked whether you are sure you want to overwrite it. For our purposes here, answer **Yes**.

Restarting or Loading a Saved City

Once you have saved a game that you want to return to, it is no longer a new game. To restart or reopen it, you use the **Load City** command. This command displays a dialog box to enable you to select the drive or directory containing the city file you wish to load. The keyboard equivalent of this command is *Ctrl-L*. If you are in the midst of a game, you will first be asked if you want to save the changes to your present city.

A city file (all city files have the extension .CTY) is loaded by double-clicking on the file name in the file loading dialog box (Figure 3.4). Alternatively, you may load the file by clicking on it once and then clicking the **Load** button, or typing the file name in the text box next to the **Load** button before clicking the **Load** button. Just above the list box is the name of the directory and drive you are in currently. The drive selector indicated by the bracketed letters **[A]**, **[B]**, **[C]**, etc., allows you to to pick the drive that contains your city files. Again, use the pointer to click on the particular drive you wish.

Try loading **Heresville** now. Select the **Load City** command, then highlight the city name in the list box of the file loading dialog box. Click the **Load** button to load **Heresville.CTY** into memory, and you should see the city name appear at the top of the Edit window.

You may at any time click the **Cancel** button or press the Esc key to exit the file loading dialog box without loading a city.

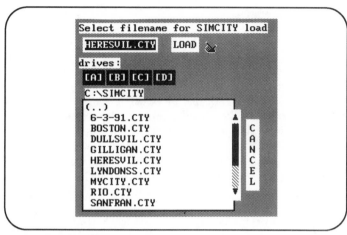

```
Select filename for SIMCITY load
HERESVIL.CTY    LOAD
drives:
[A] [B] [C] [D]
C:\SIMCITY
(..)
6-3-91.CTY                    ▲    C
BOSTON.CTY                         A
DULLSVIL.CTY                       N
GILLIGAN.CTY                       C
HERESVIL.CTY                       E
LYNDONSS.CTY                       L
MYCITY.CTY
RIO.CTY                       ▼
SANFRAN.CTY
```

Figure 3.4: The file loading dialog box

Disaster Avoidance Trick

By saving a game or scenario to disk and then reopening it, you disable the disaster that was associated with it. (This works for all disasters except for fires.) If you load the San Francisco 1906 Earthquake scenario, for example, then quickly save your game, and then use the **Load City** command to reopen it, the earthquake will never happen!

Converting Macintosh City Files to PC

If you are interested in loading onto your PC a city file that was created on a Macintosh, it is possible to open it using the **Load City** command. First, however, you must transfer the Macintosh file *via modem or serial cable* to a PC. Then you can copy the file into the directory that holds your SimCity files and load it from there using the **Load City** command. Don't bother to use the Macintosh's Apple File Exchange Utility to try to copy the file onto an MS-DOS formatted disk, and don't try to copy the file over an AppleTalk or Ethernet Network to your PC: SimCity will not recognize the file.

Loading a Scenario

There are eight scenarios that accompany SimCity. Each scenario depicts a city with a specific goal you must meet or a problem that must be solved. You have the option of starting a scenario directly from the initial road sign screen that pops up when you first start SimCity or you may start one by selecting the **Load Scenario** command from the System menu. In either case a screen of scenario choices appears when you do this (Figure 3.5). You may escape or abort this Select Scenario screen by pressing the Esc key or by clicking on the title at the top of the screen. If you select a scenario when you are already in the midst of a game, SimCity will ask you if you want to save your present city to disk before proceeding.

Pull down the System menu and select the **Load Scenario** command. You will see the Select Scenario screen, as pictured in Figure 3.5. Click on the scenario of **Dullsville** and you will soon see the city of Dullsville appear in your Edit and Maps windows.

Exiting

To exit your SimCity session and return to DOS, select the **Exit** command from the System menu. From the keyboard you may

Figure 3.5: The Select Scenario screen

instead press *Ctrl-X* to exit the program. A pop-up dialog box will first ask "Are you sure?," to which you must respond by clicking on the **Yes** button or by pressing *Y* on your keyboard if you want to exit. Make sure that you have saved your city before using this command, or you will lose your current city permanently.

Exit the program if you plan on stopping for now, otherwise keep SimCity open to follow the instructions in Step 4.

Using the File Menu on the Macintosh

Like the System menu on the PC version of SimCity, the File pull-down menu allows you to create, save, and load your city files.

Creating Your New City

If you are continuing your game from the last step, keep SimCity open and skip to the next paragraph. Otherwise, start up SimCity so that the road sign screen appears and then click on the **Start a New City** button. You will be asked to enter the name of your city and set the game play level. For now, accept the defaults and click **OK**. Once the terrain map is terraformed you will be asked the copy protection question (see Step 2). Passing the copy protection challenge allows you to view the Edit and Map windows. (If you're playing version 1.2c or 1.3c you don't have to deal with copy protection.)

Now pull down the System menu and select **Start New City**. This command starts you off with empty terrain on which you can build your city. If you are already in the midst of another city game, you will first be asked if you are sure you want to begin a different one: "New Game—Are You Sure?" Answering Yes will erase the city that is currently loaded. Answering No will continue your present city. For now, let's create a new city by answering **Yes**.

If you are not satisfied with the random terrain that is created for you when SimCity is terraforming, you may select the **Generate A New Terrain** button, and a new landscape will be terraformed. Otherwise, click the **Use This Map** button to consent to the displayed geography. You also can give your city a name, or accept the default name of **SomeWhere**, in a text box at the top of the window. The keyboard equivalent of this command on the Macintosh is the ⌘-*N* key combination. For now, accept the terrain that is displayed, by clicking the **Use This Map** button.

Next, you will be permitted to set the game play level to Easy, Medium, or Hard and to give a new name to your city. Essentially, the game play level of **Easy** starts you off with $20,000, the **Medium** level allows you $10,000, and the **Hard** level grants you a measly $5,000. At the Hard level, it is very difficult to meet the demands of a growing city and appease the Sims at the same time. The Easy level gives you more latitude and freedom to plan your city without worrying too much about lack of money. Even at the Easy level, though, you must watch your expenditures and not overspend.

Giving Your City a Name

Give your new city a new name by clicking in the city name text box and typing **SomeWhere2**. Click **OK** to confirm the name choice. Once you have passed the copy protection gauntlet (versions 1.2b&w and 1.3b&w), the Edit and Maps windows appear on your screen and you are ready to start zoning and building.

Saving Your City for Later Play

At some point you will probably want to freeze a game at a certain stage in its development so that you may return to it at a later time and start where you left off. If you are simply planning on exiting SimCity in order to get something else accomplished in your life, you need only select the **Save City** option from the File menu before exiting the program. If you want to save the game at a certain stage mainly so you can come back to it after playing through that stage—in order to compare the results of different approaches, for example—you should save the problem stage and the resulting outcome *as different files*. In order to do this, you need to use the **Save City as...** option instead of the **Save City** option.

In fact, you may find that you want to save the game at numerous points in order to try alternative approaches to a number of problems. Whenever you are interested in saving various stages or versions of the same game, be sure to use **Save City as** and to give each version a different name.

Using the Save City Option

Selecting the **Save City** menu option brings up a dialog box in which you can save the currently open game to any directory or drive of your choosing. The name of your city cannot be modified in the **Save City** dialog box, so choosing this command will only save the city with the name it already has. The keyboard equivalent for **Save City** is ⌘-*S*. Try saving your city now using either the mouse or the keyboard.

Restarting or Loading a Saved City

Once you have saved a game that you want to return to, it is no longer a new game. To restart or reopen it, you use the **Load City** command. This command displays a dialog box to enable you to select the drive or directory containing the city file you wish to load. Select the city file you wish by highlighting it, then click twice to begin loading it. (Keyboard users may use the ⌘-*L* keyboard equivalent.)

Disaster Avoidance Trick

By saving a game or scenario to disk and then reopening it, you disable the disaster that was associated with it. (This works for all disasters except for fires.) If you load the San Francisco 1906 Earthquake scenario, for example, and quickly save your game, and then use the **Load City** command to reopen it, the earthquake will never happen!

Converting PC City Files to Macintosh

If you are interested in loading onto your Macintosh a city file that was created on a PC, it is possible to open it using the **Load City** command. First, however, you must transfer the PC file *via modem or serial cable* to a Macintosh. Then you can copy the file into the directory that holds your SimCity files and load it from there using the **Load City** command. Don't bother to use the Macintosh's Apple File Exchange Utility to try and copy the file onto a Macintosh formatted disk, and don't try to convert the PC file to a Macintosh file format so that you can read it over an AppleTalk or Ethernet network: SimCity will fail to recognize the new city file.

Loading a Scenario

There are eight scenarios that accompany SimCity. Each scenario depicts a city with a specific goal you must meet or a problem that must be solved. You have the option of starting a scenario directly from the initial road sign screen that pops up when you first start SimCity or you may start one by selecting the **Load Scenario** command from the System menu. In either case a screen of scenario choices appears when you do this (Figure 3.5). You may escape or abort this Select Scenario screen by pressing the Esc key or by clicking on the title at the top of the screen. If you select a scenario when you are already in the midst of a game, SimCity will ask you if you want to save your present city to disk before proceeding.

Quitting

To exit from SimCity and return to the Desktop, select the **Quit** command. If the current game has not yet been saved, SimCity will ask you whether you wish to save it to disk before quitting. (Pressing ⌘-*Q* from the keyboard will also exit you from SimCity.) As a precaution, SimCity will first prompt you with a dialog box message asking you to confirm whether you really are sure you want to quit. Click on **Yes** to quit, and **No** if you wish to return to the game.

Exit the program if you plan on stopping for now. Otherwise keep SimCity open and proceed to the next step.

Step 4

Windows on Your World

What Is There to See?

SimCity presents all the information regarding your city in a series of five vivid graphical windows. This step will help you learn how to use these windows and understand what it is they show.

Two of the five windows—the Edit and Budget windows—allow you to actually control your city. The other three windows—the Maps, Graphs, and Evaluation windows—are passive in the sense that they only give you feedback and don't allow you to do anything. These latter windows provide essential information or other views to help guide you in your decision making. Any of the windows can be summoned by pulling down the Windows menu and selecting the window or by using a keyboard equivalent. On the Windows menu you will find the names of all five windows. In the PC version, you will also find a few window manipulation commands.

The Windows

Maps

The first time you select the **Maps** option in the Windows menu, the City Form window (on the PC) or the City Map:Comprehensive window (on the Macintosh) pops open on your desktop. Up to this point the terms "the Maps window" and "the City Map:Comprehensive window" or "the City Form window" have been essentially synonymous. The City Form or City Map:Comprehensive map is just one version of the Maps window, displaying all the physical forms and structures in your entire given region. This macroscopic view can be modified to show only certain features or patterns. For example, roads, transit lines, traffic density, population growth, fire and police department coverage, high crime areas, land values, and other areas of concern can be monitored in the same window by selecting icons that call up different versions of the main map. These specialized maps have different titles (at the top of the window), and they illustrate demographic or density information by the degree to which they are colored or shaded. A legend is provided along the lower left side of the relevant maps to help you interpret the relative weight of the different shaded or colored portions of the map.

In the Maps window is a flashing selection rectangle that you can drag via the keyboard, joystick, or mouse to reposition the Edit window's map. The rectangle is really a miniature of the Edit window, and repositioning it causes the view in the Edit window to jump to the new location. This tool is very convenient when you wish to quickly scroll or move the Edit window great distances. Step 8 goes into greater detail on the Maps window.

When the Maps window is concealed behind another window, selecting the **Maps** option will bring it to the forefront. On PCs, the keyboard equivalent of selecting the Maps window is *Ctrl-M,* or the Enter key; on the Macintosh it is ⌘-*M*.

On the PC, pressing the Enter key when in any window will open and activate the Maps window.

Graphs

By selecting the **Graphs** option on the Windows menu, you can display the Graphs window and glean valuable data on the past history of the city. Vital statistics for the city can be graphically plotted for the past 10 or 120 years. A group of icons in this window allows you to display growth patterns in pollution, crime, population, commerce, industry, and cash flow for your city. Viewing this information is helpful in spotting trends over time that would not be visible on a map.

The Graphs window, seen in Figure 4.1, can be selected from the keyboard by pressing *Ctrl-G* on the PC and ⌘-*G* on the Macintosh. Step 9 examines in detail the icon buttons and what each graph represents.

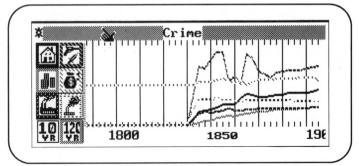

Figure 4.1: The Graphs window

Budget

The **Budget** option on the Windows menu brings up the Budget window, which provides financial information about your city and gives you control over the purse strings of City Hall. In this window, you set the property tax rate (from 0 to 20 percent) and the amount of funding for various city services. You set funding levels for the transportation, fire, and police departments as a percentage (0 to 100) of the amount that each agency requests.

Every January taxes are collected automatically. At that time the Budget window will pop up, querying you on the next year's level of spending and taxation. If you have toggled **Auto-Budget** on from the Options menu, the Budget window will not appear each year. This is because SimCity assumes that your funding and tax rates will remain at their previous settings, and that you don't want any changes (see Step 10).

Bringing up the Budget window on your desktop can also be accomplished from the keyboard by pressing *Ctrl-B* on the PC and ⌘-*B* on the Macintosh.

Edit

Selecting the **Edit** option from the Windows menu will open the Edit window. It is in this window that all zoning and building takes place. Occupying this window are many icons, several text or message boxes, window gadgets, indicators, and a large map. The map you see is a detailed enlargement of the moveable selection rectangle in the Maps window. Steps 5 and 6 introduce you to all the features of this window.

From the keyboard, you can open the Edit window by pressing *Ctrl-E* on the PC and ⌘-*E* on the Macintosh.

Evaluation

The **Evaluation** option from the Windows menu opens a window that provides feedback on your performance as mayor, census statistics, opinion polls, and your overall city score. Opening this window frequently is one of the best ways to determine whether your policies are working or not. Emigration and immigration numbers tell you whether growth is occurring, or whether the Sims are leaving in droves. Public opinion polls alert you to the Sims' biggest complaints with your city so that you can take action before it is too late. The Sims usually vote with their feet (that is, they pack up and leave if things become intolerable), but on occasion they have been known to take matters into their own hands and impeach the mayor.

Open the Evaluation window from the keyboard by pressing *Ctrl-U* on the PC, and ⌘-*U* on the Macintosh.

Getting a Handle on Your Windows

The PC version of SimCity, as mentioned before, has a few more options in the Windows menu than the Macintosh version. These additional commands allow you to close, hide, reposition, and resize certain selected windows. If you are a Macintosh user, you will not need these extra controls, since you are presumably already proficient at opening, closing, resizing, and moving windows using the mouse.

Pulling Down the Windows Menu

To pull down the Windows menu, simply click on it with the pointer. PC users can also press the *Alt-W* key combination (the *W* signifying the first letter of the menu name), or press the F5 function key.

The Windows menus for the PC and for the Macintosh appear in Figure 4.2.

Opening a Window

Open a window by selecting the window name in the Windows menu or by using keyboard equivalent, which you can see marked next to each menu option. Try opening the Graphs window now by selecting the **Graphs** menu option.

Moving Around inside a Window

Once you are in a window for the PC version of SimCity, you can use the mouse, joystick, or the + and − keys on the numeric keypad to move the pointer to important "hot spots". Hot spots are those locations in a window where you can select an icon or alter a setting. Macintosh players need only click on the hot spot or icon they wish to select. Cycle through the icons in the icon palette on the left-hand side of the Graphs window using the + key or pointer. Pick the

```
┌─────────────────────────────────────────┐
│      ▚INDOWS ▚                            │
│   ┌──────────────────────┐               │
│   │ Maps        Ctrl-M│                   │
│   │ Graphs      Ctrl-G│                   │
│   │ Budget      Ctrl-B│  ┌──────────────┐ │
│   │ Edit        Ctrl-E│  │ Windows      │ │
│   │ Evaluation  Ctrl-U│  ├──────────────┤ │
│   │ Close       Ctrl-C│  │ Maps     ⌘M │  │
│   │ Hide        Ctrl-H│  │ Graphs   ⌘G │  │
│   │ Position    Ctrl-P│  │ Budget   ⌘B │  │
│   │ Resize (Edit) Ctrl-R│ │ Edit     ⌘E │  │
│   └──────────────────────┘  │ Evaluation ⌘U │ │
│                          └──────────────┘ │
└─────────────────────────────────────────┘
```

Figure 4.2: The Windows menu: PC version (left) and Macintosh version (right)

Crime Rate icon, pictured as a pistol and a knife, by clicking on it with the space bar (PC version only), mouse, or joystick button. The **Crime Rate** icon will become highlighted and you will see the crime rate for the last 10 or 120 years displayed on a graph.

Closing a Window

Closing a window is accomplished on both the PC and Macintosh by clicking the *close box* or *close button* in the upper left-hand corner of the window. Some windows, notably the Budget window on the Macintosh and both the Budget and Evaluation windows on the PC, do not have a close box or button; however, clicking anywhere in the Evaluation window or clicking on the **Go with these figures** button in the Budget window will exit you from the window. PC users can also press *Ctrl-C* or select **Close** from the Windows menu to close any window. (**Close** as a menu option is available only on the PC.)

Close the Graphs window now by clicking on the close box or close button.

Hiding a Window

On the PC, selecting the **Hide** command under the Windows menu causes the topmost or front window to be shuffled to a position underneath all other open windows. The window that you hide is not actually closed, but it is no longer the active window, the one receiving your direct instructions. It is, rather, lying in the background, waiting to leap instantly to the foreground should you again select it. Mouse users will not bother with this feature since clicking on a window below your currently active window accomplishes the same end. (System 7 Macintosh users should not confuse this command with the **Hide** command found on the Macintosh Applications menu on the far right of the menu bar. The SimCity **Hide** command is available as a menu option only on the PC.)

To demonstrate how the **Hide** command works, let's try it on the "City Forms" Maps window that initially covers a portion of the Edit window. Select **Hide** from the Windows menu and you will immediately see the City Forms window shuffled to a position behind the Edit window—the Edit window will obscure that portion of the City Forms window that it is covering. Press *Ctrl-H* (or select **Hide** once again) to reactivate this option, and the City Forms window will reassert its former position on your desktop.

This example is for PC users only

Repositioning a Window

Macintosh users can move any window except the Budget window simply by clicking and dragging the window via the title bar. With the PC, this procedure can be performed only on the Edit, Maps, and Graphs windows.

If you are playing with the PC version and you don't have a mouse or joystick, moving a window is accomplished by selecting the **Position** option on the Windows menu and then using the cursor-movement keys to drag the window to a different location. Try this now with the Maps window. Select **Position** (or press *Ctrl-P*) and then press the arrow keys on your keyboard to move the window to a new location. A faint outline of the window will appear as you do this, giving you an idea of where the window will finally rest when you complete the move. When you are finished, press Enter or the space bar to make the window take up its new position.

Resizing a Window

Only the Edit window can be resized.

Resizing the Edit window for Macintosh users is a simple matter of clicking and dragging the *grow box,* located in the lower right corner of the Edit window. PC players can also resize this window by clicking and dragging on the *resize box,* located in the same (lower right) corner of the Edit window and marked by a + sign. There is a limit to how much you can expand or contract the Edit window, so don't get too excited.

To use the resize box, select it and then use the mouse, joystick, or cursor keys to resize the Edit window. As you are resizing the window, you will see a ghosted rectangle indicating what the new size of the window will be when you are finished. After you are satisfied with the new size, press Enter or the left mouse button to complete the transformation.

Step 5

Inspect Your Gadgets
(Special Interface Tools)

The Edit window is the place where you will find all the building and zoning tools that you use to construct and design your city. There are also a number of other gadgets and a large map area. Together, these give you total mastery over the graphical environment of SimCity. *Gadgets,* for the most part, allow you to manipulate the window or the visual aspects of the simulator, and the tool *icons* are the means by which you zone or build objects. Useful information is also displayed in some of the Edit window's gadgets, helping guide you in your decision making.

Although it is functionally equivalent, the Macintosh Edit window has a slightly different look than the PC's Edit window. Because of confusion that might arise by mixing the two, this step will describe the PC version first and the Macintosh version second. You may skip over either section of text that does not apply to your computer. This step concludes with a look at terrain features, which are shared by both PC and Mac versions.

Gadgets in the PC Edit Window

Let's look at the Edit window screen, as pictured in Figure 5.1. The figure labels should make crystal clear the names of each gadget or icon. The first gadget at the top of the window is the *title bar,* and in it you will find the city name, the city date, and the *close button.* Below the title bar is the *message bar,* which displays the amount of funds available in your treasury and any pertinent messages. Beneath the message bar is the Edit *map,* and to the immediate left of that is the *icon or tool palette.* You select the tool you want individually, according to what you want to build or zone, and then position the tool's pointer on the map. Clicking once with the mouse or joystick button (or space bar) will then cause the selected zone or object to be situated on the map. This is the primary technique by which you construct your city. Underneath the icons is the *Demand indicator.* Below this (and slightly to the right) is the *icon title box.* In the lower right corner of the Edit window you will find the *resize box,* which is used for resizing the window.

Title Bar

The title bar has two principal functions. It displays the current city date and name, and it is used to drag the Edit window around your desktop. To move the Edit window, click the pointer anywhere in the title bar and, while holding down the button or space bar, move the window to its new location.

Notice that each month of the game year is updated in the city date area of the title bar. When you speed things up through the Game Speed menu (accessed via the **Speed** option on the Options menu), the months will change more rapidly. Keep an eye on this chrono-logical instrument, so you will know how quickly the simulation is proceeding. You might discover that the game is going too slowly for you, or even, for that matter, too fast.

Close Button

Clicking the close button will close the Edit window, hiding it from your desktop. The keyboard equivalent of this command is *Ctrl-C*.

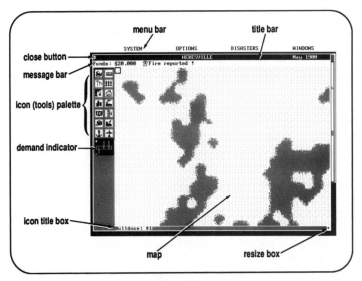

Figure 5.1: The Edit window on the PC

If you desire to redisplay the Edit window, you can either summon it from the Windows pull-down menu, or press *Ctrl-E*.

Message Bar

This important gadget is an informational tool. In the message bar you will find how much money you have left in the treasury, and be able to read messages sent by the Sims or by the simulator. If you click on the message bar, the last message that was sent will be redisplayed.

Messages sent by the simulator include disaster warnings, population updates, and complaints from the Sims themselves. Problems such as unemployment, brownouts, heavy traffic, insufficient funds, or such needs as more parks, commercial zones, housing, or industry, are all brought to your attention in this area. From time to time, a more formal text box will pop up on your screen giving you a detailed synopsis of what's wrong, or more importantly, congratulating you on a job well done.

When a disaster or traffic problem occurs somewhere in your city, a **GOTO** button looking like an eye with the word "Go" underneath will appear in the message bar alongside a message informing you of the nature of the trouble. Usually a sound of some sort will be heard preceding the message announcement. For example, if the message concerns a traffic jam, you will first hear the sound of a helicopter and the voice of a traffic reporter warning you of heavy traffic ("Sky One reporting heavy traffic"). You would next see the **GOTO** button in the message bar accompanied by the traffic warning message. Clicking on the button takes you directly to the scene, where you can then attempt to resolve the situation.

The GOTO button

Keyboard users can activate the **GOTO** button by pressing the Tab key. If you wish to return to the location where you were before you executed the **GOTO** command, simply press the Tab key a second time.

If you have toggled on **Auto-Goto** under the Options menu, you needn't concern yourself with the **GOTO** button, since you will automatically be transported to any trouble area without any manual intervention.

Tool Icons

From the palette of tool icons, you select a tool to zone new areas, to bulldoze, or to build new infrastructure. Tools that are unavailable due to lack of funds are greyed or ghosted out. You can select an icon by pointing and clicking using the pointer, or by using the + or − keys on the numeric keypad to cycle forwards or backwards in the palette. Step 6 goes into greater detail on the functional use of each icon.

Demand Indicator

Just below the icon tools palette is the Demand indicator, which tells you whether there is a positive or negative demand for Residential (R), Commercial (C), and Industrial (I) zones. This three-column bar chart graphically shows, by the length and direction of each bar, the need for each type of zone. When a zone bar points up (positive direction), there is a pent-up demand for that type of zone, and this should be a cue to start putting new zones in your city. When a zone bar points down (negative direction), there is an overabundance of that zone type and you can take that as a sign not to build any more.

Note that there is often a time lag or delay involved while the simulator updates all the zones, so you will not necessarily see instantaneously accurate zone demands. Use this indicator as a guide, don't respond with a knee-jerk reaction to every quiver of the chart.

Icon Title Box

Each icon that you elect to use will cost you money. The icon title box will tell you the name of the currently selected icon and how much it will cost to use that tool in one tile or zone.

Resize Box

Resizing the Edit window can be accomplished in one of two ways. You can select the **Resize (Edit)** command (*Ctrl-R* from the keyboard) from the Windows menu, or you can click and drag on the resize box located in the lower right corner of the Edit window. (See Step 4 for instructions on how to use the **Resize (Edit)** command in the Windows menu.) By holding down the mouse or joystick button (or the space bar) while the pointer is on the resize box you can redraw the window's borders to a new size. There is a certain minimum and maximum size to which you can scale the Edit window, so don't expect to shrink it down to the size of an icon or expand it to fill the screen of a two-page monitor.

Scrolling

You can scroll inside the Edit window using several different methods:

Scrolling with the Pointer

By moving the hand pointer with the mouse, joystick, or keyboard so that it touches one of the four edges of your monitor's screen, you can scroll in the direction that you have moved the pointer. For example, if you move the pointer up so that it is going off the edge of the top menu bar, it will appear as though the window is moving in the same direction, showing you more of the map above the Edit window. Likewise, moving the pointer off the right side of the screen will scroll to the right.

Scrolling with the Joystick

Joystick users have an alternative way of scrolling without having to move the pointer to the edge of the screen. Just hold down the Ctrl key and move the joystick in the direction you wish to scroll.

If you find to your annoyance that you're scrolling every time you try to move the pointer to an item *near* the edge of the window, take heart. You can easily disable the pointer's scrolling function in the Edit window by pressing the ScrollLock key on your keyboard. With ScrollLock on, scrolling can then only be accomplished by using the Ctrl key in combination with your keyboard's cursor-movement keys.

Scrolling from the Keyboard

Remember that if you need to use the numeric keypad's arrow keys, *you must always keep the NumLock key in the off position.* Failure to do so will prevent you from using the pointer and scrolling the map via that part of the keyboard.

To scroll using the keyboard, press the Ctrl key and, while still holding it down, press one of the arrow keys to scroll in the corresponding direction.

Scrolling Using the Maps Window's Selection Rectangle

The quickest way to scroll your map over large distances is to switch to the Maps window and move the flashing selection rectangle in the direction you want to go. The mouse, joystick, or keyboard can be used to reposition the rectangle over the part of the city that you want to focus on in the Edit window. While the rectangle is being moved, you should notice how the Edit window's map rapidly changes to reflect its new location.

Gadgets in the Mac's Edit Window

As mentioned before, the Edit window's gadgets for the Macintosh version of SimCity are, for the most part, functionally equivalent to the PC's gadgets. You will notice that the names of all the gadgets and controls are clearly labeled. At the top of the window you can see the *title bar,* which contains the city name, the *close box*, the *zoom box*, the *joystick box*, and the *total funds & messages bar.* Below the title bar is the Edit *map,* and to the immediate left is the *icon or tool palette.* You select the tool you want individually, according to what you want to build or zone, and then position the tool's pointer on the map. Clicking once will then cause the se-lected zone or object to be situated on the map. This is the primary technique by which you construct your city. Underneath the icons is the *Demand indicator,* and below this is the *selected item & cost box.* In the lower right corner of the Edit window, you will find the *grow box,* which is used for resizing the window. The right and bottom edges of the Edit window contain the Macintosh's ubiquitous scroll bars, used to scroll the map in the Edit window. Figure 5.2 shows the Edit window along with labels to identify all the gadgets.

Title Bar

The title bar has two principal functions. It displays information such as the current city date and name (and includes the total funds & messages bar), and it is used to drag the Edit window around your desktop. To move the Edit window, click the pointer anywhere in the title bar and, while holding down the button or space bar, move the window to its new location.

Notice that each month of the game year is updated in the city date area of the Title Bar. When you speed things up through the Game Speed menu, the months will change more rapidly. Keep an eye on

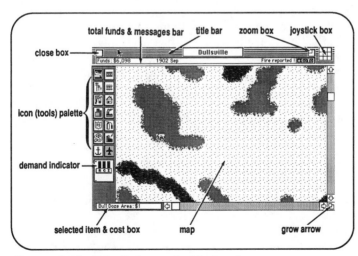

Figure 5.2: The Edit window on the Macintosh

this chronological instrument, so you will know how quickly the simulation is proceeding. You might discover that the game is going too slowly for you, or even, for that matter, too fast.

Close Box

Clicking the close box in the upper left corner will close the Edit window, hiding it from your desktop. If you want to redisplay the Edit window, you can select it from the Windows pull-down menu, or press ⌘-*E*.

Zoom Box

Clicking on the zoom box in the upper right (almost in the corner) allows you to expand the Edit window to fill the entire screen. Clicking it again will return the window to its former size.

Joystick Box

This little three-by-three grid in the upper right corner acts like a real joystick and allows you to scroll the Edit window in any direction. Because it allows you to scroll diagonally as well as vertically and horizontally, it is extremely useful. To use the joystick box move the pointer onto one of the outside squares (the middle square does not scroll) and hold the mouse button down. As long as you hold the button down, you can scroll the Edit window in the corresponding direction. For instance, to scroll diagonally down to the left, move the pointer to the lower left corner square in the joystick box. To scroll straight up, move the pointer to the top middle square.

Total Funds & Messages Bar

This important gadget is an informational tool. In the message bar you will find how much money you have left in the treasury, and be able to read messages sent by the Sims or by the simulator. If you click on the message bar, the last message that was sent will be redisplayed.

Messages sent by the simulator include disaster warnings, population updates, and complaints from the Sims themselves. Problems such as unemployment, brownouts, heavy traffic, insufficient funds, or such needs as more parks, commercial zones, housing, or industry, are all brought to your attention in this area. From time to time, a more formal text box will pop up on your screen giving you a detailed synopsis of what's wrong, or, more importantly, congratulating you on a job well done.

When a disaster or traffic problem occurs somewhere in your city, a **GOTO** button will appear in the far right of the message bar alongside a message informing you of the nature of the trouble. Usually a sound of some sort will be heard preceding the message announcement. For example, if the message concerns a traffic jam, you will first hear the sound of a helicopter and the voice of a traffic reporter warning you of heavy traffic ("Sky One reporting heavy traffic"). You would next see the **GOTO** button in the message bar accompanied by the traffic warning message. Clicking on the button takes you directly to the scene, where you can then attempt to resolve the situation.

If you have toggled on **Auto-Goto** under the Options menu, you needn't concern yourself with the **GOTO** button, since you will automatically be transported to any trouble area without manual intervention.

Tool Icons

From the palette of icons, you select a tool to zone new areas, to bulldoze, or to build new infrastructure. Tools that are unavailable due to lack of funds are greyed or ghosted out. Step 6 goes into greater detail on the functional use of each icon.

Demand Indicator

Just below the icon tools palette is the Demand indicator, which tells you whether there is a positive or negative demand for Residential (R), Commercial (C), and Industrial (I) zones. This three-column bar chart graphically shows, by the length and direction of each bar, the need for each type of zone. When a zone bar points up (positive direction), there is a pent-up demand for that type of zone, and this should be a cue to start putting new zones in your city. When a zone bar points down (negative direction), there is an overabundance of that zone type and you can take this as a sign not to build any more.

Note that there is often a time lag or delay involved while the simulator updates all the zones, so you will not necessarily see instantaneously accurate zone demands. Use this indicator as a guide, don't respond with a knee-jerk reaction to every quiver of the chart.

Selected Item & Cost Box

Each icon tool that you elect to use will cost you money. The Selected Item & Cost box will tell you the name of the currently selected icon and how much it will cost to use.

Grow Box

The grow box allows you to resize the Edit window by clicking and dragging with the mouse pointer. To do this, click and hold down the mouse button while the pointer is over the grow box. If you want to enlarge the window, continue to hold the mouse button down and move the pointer diagonally outward. If you want to reduce the window, move the pointer diagonally inward. When you release the mouse button, the Edit window's borders will be redrawn to the new size.

Scroll Bars

Macintosh users should have no trouble at all understanding how to use the vertical and horizontal scroll bars. Simply click and drag the scroll box within the scroll bar or click on the scroll arrows to scroll the Edit window.

Terrain Features (Macintosh and PC)

The terrain you see in the Edit and Map windows is of three different types: open land, forests, and water. These can be readily identified by their shade or color depending on whether you have a monochrome or color monitor. In addition to natural terrain, there are a few tile markers that indicate that an extraordinary event is taking place. These include rubble from demolished zones and buildings, radioactive contamination, flooding, fire, and tornados. These are all shown in Figure 5.3.

Open Land

Any area that is colored brown on a color monitor or a light shade with speckles on a monochrome monitor is open land. Since it is

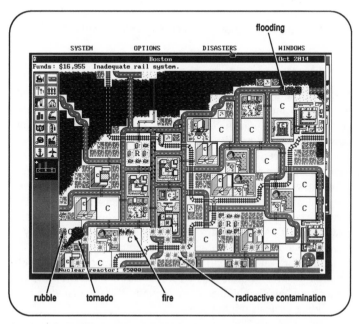

Figure 5.3: Rubble, radioactive contamination, flooding, fire and tornado tiles as seen in the Edit window

devoid of any surface features, Open Land does not require any bulldozing before zoning or building commences. Any land or zone that you bulldoze clear will become open land. Note that land values are higher for open land that is near water or near forests and parks.

Trees and Forests

Any area that is colored green on a color monitor or a medium shade on a monochrome monitor is trees and forests. This land must first be bulldozed into open land before zoning or building can occur. If you have enabled **Auto-Bulldoze** in the Options menu then you need not worry about bulldozing forest land before zoning or building; the bulldozing will be taken care of automatically when you first go to zone or build. Keep in mind that higher property or land values are attributable to the proximity of forests, so don't clearcut your forests without a darned good reason. High land values are the key to building successful cities in SimCity.

Water

Water is displayed in blue on color monitors or in a darker shade than forests on monochrome monitors. Roads and railroads that cross water are automatically built as bridges and subways, and power lines automatically cross in underwater cables. Roads, railroads, and power lines all share the common trait that they cannot have bends, curves, turns or intersections while traversing water. Shorelines can be extended by one tile into water by bulldozing water tiles that are adjacent to land. The intended effect of this action is that you are dumping landfill in the shore areas to create new land. With **Auto-Bulldoze** enabled (in the Options menu), you can place a zone or building on a shore so that it is slightly straddling the water line and have the simulator automatically bulldoze the landfill into the water before you build. Otherwise, you must first manually bulldoze those sections of water that your zone or building projects might overlap.

Rubble

Land that has had zones or buildings bulldozed, burned, or damaged is not open land, because there is still rubble left from the demolition. Rubble appears as a roughly patterned shaded area.

Radioactive Contamination

When land has been contaminated by radiation from a nuclear power plant meltdown, it is shown with a radiation symbol. Such land cannot be used for the remainder of the game (at least 1000 SimCity years).

Flooding

Appearing as speckled water tiles, floods move along coastal areas, first occupying shoreline and then receding.

Fire

The fire tile looks like a flame. Fires are usually the indirect result of another disaster.

Tornado

Although strictly speaking tornados are not considered as a terrain feature, they nonetheless have a distinctive appearance that bears mentioning. Tornados have a nasty habit of turning up if you bulldoze churches.

Step 6

Zoning and Building

Most of the interaction you will have in SimCity takes place in the Edit window using the tool icons. This step guides you through the fourteen icon tools, acquainting you with their use and misuse.

How to Zone and Build

You zone and build in SimCity by selecting and positioning the icons from the Edit window's icon palette, located on the left side of the Edit window. Each icon represents a particular zone or object that you may wish to build, and must be moved to the map portion of the window, where you place it by clicking with the mouse or by pressing Enter. A zone or building doesn't really become activated, however, until it is electrically powered and served by some form of transportation.

Your job of planning must also include construction of an infrastructure to support the people and the economy. Although you will have your hands full managing current demands, you will also need to plan for the future needs of SimCity. Looking into your crystal ball, you must craftily predict what the future may hold, realizing that you must not overreach your means by overextending yourself with grandiose projects that may never materialize. Start frugally by building and zoning cautiously, not by splattering zones all over the map. Once these "building blocks" are in place, your city begins to grow and prosper. The challenge is to efficiently manage the growth of the city, allowing room for expansion without going broke, or letting the city manage you. Keep in mind that there are downturns in the economy over which you have no control, and to weather these periodic recessions you must not deplete your treasury. You don't want to be in the position of always responding to problems; rather, you want to have the upper hand in directing city evolution.

Using the Icons from the Palette

This next section describes the fourteen icons that make up the icon palette, discussing how they are selected and what they do. It also offers tips for using them.

Selection Techniques

An icon is selected by pointing and clicking the pointer on the icon so that it becomes highlighted. PC keyboard users can use the + and − keys on the numeric keypad to cycle through the icon choices, stopping on the icon to be selected. Once the icon has been highlighted, the pointer in the Edit window will assume the shape of a rectangle, the size of which tells you how much clear land the object or zone will take up on the Edit map. As mentioned previously, unless **Auto-Bulldoze** from the Options menu is on, you will need to bulldoze to clear any non-empty land before building or zoning can take place in that location.

The Icon Palette

Icons that are unavailable due to lack of funds appear ghosted or grayed out in the icon palette. You cannot select or activate ghosted icons, nor can you view a ghosted icon's name and cost in the icon title box. Figure 6.1 shows the Icon palette along with each icon's name.

Bulldozer

Just as the name implies, the Bulldozer is used to clear land containing buildings, forest, zones, roads, or rubble so that you can build or zone. Bulldozing simulates the preparatory work that goes into grading and excavating a site before construction can begin. If the **Auto-Bulldoze** feature from the Options menu is enabled, bulldozing will be performed automatically for you when you put in new zones, roads, rails or buildings. Otherwise, you must manually bulldoze clear each and every non-empty land tile you plan to build or zone upon.

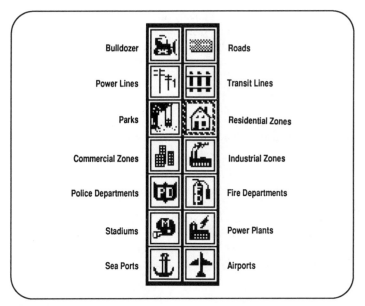

Bulldozer			Roads
Power Lines			Transit Lines
Parks			Residential Zones
Commercial Zones			Industrial Zones
Police Departments			Fire Departments
Stadiums			Power Plants
Sea Ports			Airports

Figure 6.1: The icon palette

With **Auto-Bulldoze** toggled on, you don't need to use the bulldozer to clear forests, parks (except park tiles with water fountains), power lines, or shoreline before building or zoning. (The manual incorrectly states that **Auto-Bulldoze** will clear roads or rails; you must still manually bulldoze roads and rails regardless of whether **Auto-Bulldoze** is on.)

The cost for bulldozing one small square section, or "tile," of land is one dollar. Demolition of existing zones also costs only one dollar and is accomplished by placing the square Bulldozer pointer in the middle of the zone and clicking, but the resulting rubble will cost an additional nine dollars to clear. You will be charged the same amount whether you auto-bulldoze or not. Auto-bulldozing is thus a real convenience, saving you the aggravation of tedious housekeeping tasks that are better left to the computer.

Bulldozing is also useful for clearing rubble after disasters, plowing fire breaks, filling in shoreline, and redeveloping urban areas.

If you are unfamiliar with SimCity, it will be helpful to go through the steps in using the Bulldozer. Once you know how to use this tool, you can easily translate this ability to any of the other tools on the palette.

Steps for Using the Bulldozer:

1. Select or click the Bulldozer tool on the icon palette using the mouse or joystick button or the space bar on the PC keyboard.

2. Move the pointer to the map portion of the Edit window, observing that the pointer turns into a small hollow square.

3. Find some forested land and situate the square pointer on it.

4. Bulldoze that section clear by pressing the mouse or joystick button or the space bar. That section should now be featureless, signifying open or empty terrain.

5. Bulldozing more than one section or tile of land at a time can be done by holding down the mouse or joystick button or the space bar while you move the square pointer. Drag the pointer over any land or object that you want bulldozed and it will either vanish or disappear into a pile of rubble. In effect, you are "bulldozing on the fly," using the Bulldozer as if it were an eraser.

Regardless of which icon you have selected in the PC version of SimCity, if you press the right mouse button, you will activate the Bulldozer and can immediately begin bulldozing. Pressing the left mouse button after this will reactivate the previous tool.

Roads

It costs $10 to lay each section of road. Each bridge segment costs $50. In addition, there are yearly maintenance costs, which you must pay for out of your budget in order to keep your roads and bridges in good working order. Roads must be funded at the rate of $1 for each section, and bridges at the rate of $4 per section. If you don't maintain transportation links, they will deteriorate and must be rebuilt.

Roads need touch only one side of a zone in order to have complete transportation coverage for the entire zone. It is unnecessary and financially wasteful to encircle all four sides of the zone. Be conscious of the polluting effect roads have on nearby zones. Traffic will always expand to fill available capacity, no matter how wide you build your roads.

There are a few general rules for building roads. If you build a road over water, it automatically becomes a bridge. Curves, turns, and intersections over water are prohibited, although there is a trick around this restriction (see Step 13). If you don't have **Auto-Bull-doze** toggled on, you must bulldoze trees and shoreline prior to building roads and bridges. Roads must cross over power lines and rails at right angles and cannot cross zones or buildings, with the exception of bulldozed edges of residential zones.

Steps for Building Roads:

1. With the pointer, select the Roads icon to the right of the Bulldozer icon.

2. Move the pointer to the Edit map, observing that the pointer assumes a hollow square shape.

3. Build one segment of road by clicking with the mouse or joystick button or the space bar. You should see a road tile appear on the Edit map.

4. Move the pointer one square directly to the right and click once more. The two sections should join together.

5. Pave some more segments of road adjoining the previous road tiles. Try to create one continuous stretch of road by clicking and dragging the pointer slowly. If you have any gaps, go back and fill them in.

6. To build a curve, position the Road pointer at right angles to the last road section and then click. A curved section of road should appear in the previous road tile, connecting up the road so that it is now oriented in a different direction.

7. Build a bridge by moving the Road pointer to a nearby shoreline and clicking. You must start a bridge from a

Building bridges

shore, as if you were first building the approaches. If
Auto-Bulldoze is enabled you should see your first road
segment; otherwise you must bulldoze the shoreline before
you can start bridge construction. Click again over the
water and you should see the first portion of your bridge
appearing on pylons or piers (Figure 6.2). Proceed in this
fashion until you get to the other side of the water.

Sometimes while building a long stretch of straight road, you will
find it convenient to use the Shift key in combination with clicking
and dragging the Road pointer. This constrains the road to a straight
path. Be aware that any curves or intersections cause traffic bottlenecks, so it is to your advantage to have nice straight roads for un-
restricted traffic flow.

Power Lines

Power lines are needed to electrically connect all zones and buildings with your power plants. Without electricity, your zones cannot

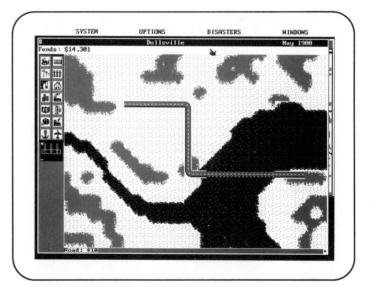

Figure 6.2: Roads over water must be straight

develop; nor can your buildings function. Zones or buildings which are unpowered appear with a flashing power symbol in the Edit window, indicating that they need to be linked up with powered zones. Zones can touch other zones and transmit power without power lines, but to connect zones that do not touch, you must use the Power Lines icon to build power lines between powered and unpowered zones and buildings. At more complex levels of the game, there is often a time lag between the time you link up the zone and the disappearance of the flashing symbol. This need not concern you untowardly, but you should be aware of it, especially as the city gets bigger and it takes longer to update each zone.

You can build power lines over forests, parks (without fountains), and shoreline if you have activated **Auto-Bulldoze** or if you have bulldozed the land clear before constructing the power line. Power lines can only cross roads and rails at right angles, and cannot cross zones. On land, they can have junctions, corners, and turns. When crossing water, power lines are laid as an underwater cable, which cannot curve or have intersections and which must cross at right angles to the shore. Step 13 describes a trick to foil the no-turns-over-water restriction.

The cost for building a power line is $5 for each land section and $25 for each underwater section. There is no yearly maintenance charge for servicing the network.

Build a power line the way you would a road. Select the Power Line icon immediately below the Bulldozer on the Icon palette, then click and drag the pointer in the map portion of the window, over the path you wish to create the power line. Before they can conduct power, power lines must touch the edge of a powered zone or building or the power plant itself.

If you are building long-distance power transmission lines, it may be helpful to use the Shift key in combination with clicking and dragging the Power Line pointer. This method constrains the power line to a straight line, making it easier to connect zones in a direct line. By connecting zones more directly you minimize transmission inefficiencies due to extra line length.

Transit Lines

The Transit Lines icon, located directly underneath the Roads icon, is used to build rails for a rapid transit system. SimCity has a built-in bias for rails in alleviating traffic congestion and reducing pollution, so it is to your advantage to build rails instead of roads wherever possible. Keep in mind, however, that it is more costly to build and maintain rails than it is to build roads. Rails have the same basic restrictions as roads. When crossing water, rails automatically run in underwater tunnels, which appear as dashed lines on your map.

Once you have laid some track, you will see a single train, moving from one end to another. Regardless of how many independent rail systems you build, you will see only one train on the map at a time—but don't worry, all areas immediately adjacent to the tracks will be adequately served.

Transit lines cost $20 to build over land and $100 for tunnels underwater. Yearly maintenance costs are $4 for each section of track and $10 for each section of underwater tunnel. Although rails are environmentally preferable compared to roads, they are frightfully expensive to maintain. To keep costs down, plan your tunnel and rail lines to be as direct and short as possible. Also, be aware that you need touch only one side of any zone with rails to have complete coverage for the entire zone. It is unnecessary to encircle all four sides of the zone.

If you have complaints from the Sims about traffic, bulldoze the clogged roads and replace them with rails using the Transit Lines icon. This will quickly solve your traffic congestion woes, and will have the added benefit of reducing pollution. Avoid the temptation of building roads side by side with rails in a parallel line. It does not reduce road traffic and is wasteful because you are not allowing zones to have access to both sides of the transportation corridor.

Building long stretches of straight track is fairly easy if you hold down the Shift key while clicking and dragging the Transit Lines pointer. The track will be constrained to either a vertical or horizontal straight line, depending on which direction you are moving the pointer.

Parks

The Parks icon is used to build or landscape parks on clear land. Selecting this icon will give you a bulldozer-sized square pointer which you then click on in the Edit map to build parks. Don't be fooled into thinking that parks are frills that you can dispense with for your city. They are extremely beneficial because they raise land values of nearby zones, indirectly increasing population, lowering crime, and, more importantly, boosting tax collections. Parks are also useful for reducing housing densities in residential zones. To do this, you bulldoze one or more corners of a residential zone and then quickly replace it with a park. The residential zone will never fully develop into a higher density zone until the park is removed.

Each park tile costs $10 to landscape and there are no yearly maintenance fees.

By holding down the Shift key while clicking and dragging the Parks pointer over the map, you can build linear swaths of park. This gives you precise control over placement of park tiles when you are concerned about space limitations on the map.

Follow the next few steps in building a park:

1. Select the Parks icon just below the Power Lines icon. (It looks like a tree with a Sim kid on a swing.)

2. Move the Parks square pointer to any clear terrain and click with the mouse or joystick button or the space bar to build your first park.

3. Holding down the Shift key to constrain park building to a straight line, click and drag the pointer in a horizontal direction. Double back underneath the top line of parks so that you have a rectangular strip of parks. You should see that in some of the park tiles there are fountains which appear at random.

Residential Zones

Residential zones take up nine tiles of empty land and are primarily used to create areas where the Sims can build homes, apartment buildings, schools, churches, and hospitals. There are four different density levels and four different land values for a zone to evolve into. The density levels go from sparse to low and then medium to high, reflecting how populated a zone is. Visually you will see this by whether you have single-family dwellings or high-rise buildings cropping up in the zone. Land values for the PC version range from *low* to *medium* to *high* to *high!*. For the Macintosh version the equivalent values are *slums, lower middle class, upper middle class,* and *upper class*. If you are interested in spurring growth in residential zones, it is helpful to zone them so that at least two or three other residential zones are touching. Zones that are by themselves tend to stabilize at lower densities.

Churches and hospitals

When you first build a zone, it can become a purely residential zone, or it can become a church or hospital. Unfortunately churches and hospitals contribute no taxes and are usually of low land value—would *you* like to live across the street from a hospital? SimCity has a predetermined formula that takes into account the number of zones you have and figures out whether your next residential zone should be a church or hospital. This ratio of residences to churches and hospitals changes during the course of the game, and although you don't have any control over when they appear, there are certain tricks to move them to less desirable areas (see step 13).

Try not to be tempted to bulldoze churches in the PC version of SimCity. You will be swiftly punished by a tornado that sweeps through your city, destroying all in its path. See Step 13 for tips on how to avoid this form of divine retribution.

The cost to build one residential zone is $100, which does not include the cost of bulldozing non-empty land before the zone can be installed.

You can selectively bulldoze single tiles within residential zones to make way for parks, roads, rails, or even other zones. One interesting application of this feature lies in creating a single-family residential zone that can never evolve into higher densities. By bulldozing a corner of a residential zone and building a park, you create a zone that will stabilize at the single-family level. This results in lower housing costs, lower population, and less traffic. Note that bulldozing a single tile only works if you bulldoze the residential zone before it has evolved from single-family dwellings to higher-density apartment buildings.

Another interesting bulldozing technique with residential zones has the opposite effect of increasing density. This is done by bulldozing clear one entire side of a residential zone, and then terracing or overlapping a second zone on top of the evacuated section. Figure 6.3 demonstrates the example of achieving lower densities by building a park in a zone and the technique of attaining higher densities by overlapping zones. The two zones occupy less space than if they were side by side, yet each zone can still fulfill its destiny. The net effect of this is that you are squeezing more density out of your

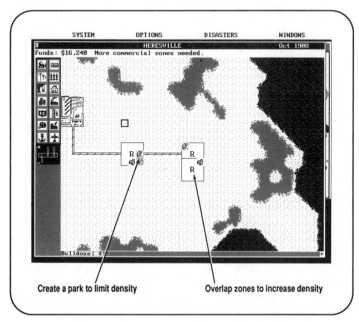

Create a park to limit density   Overlap zones to increase density

Figure 6.3: Low-density and high-density residential zones

limited land space. For the Macintosh version of SimCity, it is sometimes impossible to bulldoze an entire side of a zone. Just overlap the zones where you can.

Commercial Zones

Commercial zones are needed in SimCity for the proper development of the economy. These zones take up nine tiles of land and represent the areas where retail stores, office buildings, parking garages, gas stations, and other commercial enterprises are located. In order to prosper, a commercial zone must be powered and linked up via road or rail to a nearby residential zone. Early on in a game, you will need fewer commercial zones than you will industrial, because you will be trying to build a strong export-based economy. Later on, however, the roles are reversed and you will need more commercial zones than industrial to help fuel a robust internal economy. As with residential zones, commercial zones have a range of different land values and densities. There are 5 zone densities and 4 different land values, making a total of 20 zone possibilities.

Build a commercial zone by selecting the icon depicting three highrise office buildings (just underneath the Parks icon) and then pointing and clicking the pointer to create the zone. For the zone to develop properly, you must build transportation access and provide power. Zoning one commercial zone costs $100, not counting the bulldozing to clear the land, and there are no yearly maintenance costs.

Industrial Zones

Early on in the evolution of your city, you will want to create an export-based economy based on manufacturing durable goods. Encouraging industrial development will fuel the engine of economic growth, adding new jobs, attracting Sims to move into your city, and enhancing your tax base. However, later in the life cycle of your city, you will need fewer industrial zones and more commercial zones as you move into a post-industrial service-based economy. The downside of building industrial zones is that they inevitably cause pollution, depress land values, and increase crime. They are vital, though, for helping to create a thriving city. There are eight varieties of industrial zone types, broken down into four industrial density classes (low to high), and two land value types (low and high).

You build an industrial zone the way you would a residential or commercial zone; that is, you select the icon resembling a factory belching black soot (just below the Residential Zone icon) and then click where you want the zone to be located. You must furnish power and transportation for the zone to develop normally. Zoning one industrial zone costs $100, not counting any bulldozing that may be needed to clear the nine tiles the zone occupies. There are no yearly maintenance fees.

Police Departments

The Police Department icon, resembling a police badge with the initials PD, is used to build a police station to combat crime. Police stations have the added benefit of bolstering nearby property values, due to their crime-deterrent effect. As with other zones and buildings, police stations must be electrically connected and have transportation links in order for them to affect the areas they serve. If you are trying to increase population and you have a crime problem, building police departments to suppress crime can dramatically improve growth. Too many stations, on the other hand, can severely drain the coffers of your city treasury by their yearly funding demands. To maximize the performance of your police station coverage, try placing them in a checkerboard pattern on your map. This way they will not overlap covered territory with an unnecessary duplication of services.

Building a police station costs $500, and the yearly cost to maintain it is $100. Reducing the percentage funding for police stations affects their coverage area commensurately, thereby increasing criminal activity. If you reduce funding too much, the simulator will alert you with a message telling you that the "Police department needs more funding."

To build a police station, select the Police Department badge icon below the Commercial Zones icon to begin construction. Move the square pointer to the area that you wish to place the station and then click. A blue building with a flashing power symbol and the initials PD should appear. Connect up the power and link the department to your transportation network. You will now have police protection services for an area extending several zones away in all directions. The strength of the coverage is proportionate to how close the zone is to the station.

Fire Departments

As a result of natural or unnatural disasters, fires may break out in your city. The Fire Department icon, resembling a fire extinguisher, is used to build fire stations to deal with fire threats. You use this tool in the same way as the Police Department icon, allowing for transportation access and power line connections to activate fire protection services. Again, maximum efficiencies are achieved if you build fire stations in a checkerboard pattern so that there is no useless duplication of coverage territory.

The need for fire stations can be totally eliminated if you toggle on the **Disable** option (PC version) or the **No Disasters** option (Macintosh version) from the Disasters menu. This way you can save yourself a great deal of money and grief, and also have the satisfaction of knowing how clever you are. If you are a SimCity "purist," however, this method may not strike you as a fair challenge. A second method of saving money by not building fire stations is to just bulldoze fire breaks around fires whenever they occur. In order to do this you must bulldoze clear all tiles surrounding a fire. This includes roads, tracks, power lines, zones, buildings, and rubble.

The cost to establish a fire station is $500, and it costs an additional $100 each year to properly fund it. A reduction of funding results in an impaired ability to cope with fires: the effective radius of containment is reduced, and fires farther away may burn unchecked, possibly turning into infernos.

Stadiums

To promote domestic tranquility, you must provide entertainment for your subjects. If you don't do this they may become bored, discontented, and restless, and may start clamoring for your head. As ancient Rome discovered almost twenty centuries ago, and modern America today, entertainment is one of the main things a city can provide to placate the populace and divert their attention from civic problems. As long as the citizenry are well fed and entertained (panem et circenses), and not angered too much, your position as Mayor is solid. When the time comes for you to build a stadium, the Sims will send you a subtle message: "Residents demand a stadium." You build the stadium by selecting the Stadium icon, which looks like a football helmet, and then pointing and clicking on the spot where you want the stadium. Note that, unlike other zones or buildings, stadiums take up more space by using 16 tiles of land. One stadium is about all you need for a city.

Bread and Circuses

Interestingly enough, stadiums, like airports and sea ports, can be placed anywhere on the map and will act as a catalyst for increasing residential growth and tax revenue. However, if they are located in close proximity to residential zones, they seem to encourage even more development. Just be sure that the stadium is powered and that there is adequate transportation access.

The cost to build a stadium is $3,000. There are no yearly maintenance costs.

Power Plants

Without power, zones and buildings in SimCity cannot function and will eventually wither away. The Power Plants icon, resembling a building being struck by lightning, allows you to build either a nuclear or coal-fired power plant to supply electricity. When you select this icon, a submenu pops up giving you the choice between the nuclear and coal power plant. Use the pointer or arrow keys to select the type you prefer and then click to activate the selection; then place the pointer where you want to build and click. If you have chosen the coal-fired plant, you will immediately see a large building with tall smokestacks billowing smoke. Otherwise, for the nuclear plant, you will see a large building with an atom symbol prominently displayed. Your next step is to build power lines to connect unpowered zones and buildings to the plant.

There are advantages and disadvantages to each type of plant. Nuclear power plants are costly ($5,000), but can supply enough power for 150 zones. Unfortunately, nuclear power plants also carry the slight risk of catastrophic meltdown, which can contaminate vast tracts of land, rendering them unfit for habitation. Coal power plants, on the other hand, are safer and cheaper, costing only $3,000, but they can supply only enough power for 30 zones and are heavy polluters. In SimCity's simple model, nuclear power is favored as a clean and environmentally benign energy source, while coal power is denigrated as a dirty and polluting source of energy. SimCity has a built-in bias towards nuclear power; therefore it is advantageous to build nuclear power plants rather than coal-powered plants.

When you exceed the number of zones that your power plant can handle, you will get a message warning of brownouts and telling you to build more power plants. On the Edit map, zones and buildings that are without power will appear with flashing power symbols in their center.

Sea Ports

Sea ports have little economic impact on small cities, but for larger cities they help to accelerate the growth of industrial zones. Ideally, in the real world, you would build a sea port on a shoreline situated near industry, but SimCity program doesn't care where you place them; you can build them in the middle of the desert if you want to. (SimCity just checks to see if a sea port exists and whether it is powered or not). Separating residential zones from sea ports is a good idea because of the heavy pollution that the port creates.

Constructing a sea port costs $5,000 and there are no yearly mainte-nance costs. To build a sea port, select the Sea Ports icon (the anchor) and move the square pointer until it rests over the sea port's proposed new location. Click the pointer and you will see a shipping port, 16 tiles in size, appear on the map. After hooking the port up to the power grid, the sea port will become active and you will hear the sounds of a ship navigating some nearby waters. Scrolling the map to view the waterways will reveal a single ship somewhere in the water.

Airports

Airports are the largest building type, occupying 36 land tiles, and are also the most expensive, costing $10,000 to build. They are best built after you have a large city with plenty of commercial zones. Commercial growth will tend to stabilize at a certain level without the introduction of an airport, so if you notice stagnant commercial zone activity, it is time to build an airport. There are no yearly maintenance costs associated with airports.

You build an airport by selecting the Airports icon and positioning the pointer over the land area where the airport is to be placed. Click to build the airport and then connect it up to the power line network. Very shortly, you will see a radar dish rotating in the airport, and somewhere on your map a plane will be making its final approach. A traffic helicopter will also appear, constantly interrupting you with nitwit traffic reports. To save your sanity, turn off the sound under the Options menu.

As with other public works facilities, SimCity doesn't care where you place your airport. But if you want to create a buffer zone to protect you against air crashes, build your airport on a peninsula, island, or any waterfront area (or place it in the boonies far away from urban development). That way when a plane crashes, it decreases the chance of destroying a zone. Another precaution you can take is to build a fire department next to the airport. Any crashes and fires will be quickly dealt with. Or, if you are so inclined, you can select the **Disable** option (**No Disasters** option on the Macintosh) under the Disasters menu, and you will never have to worry about air crashes or fires. Airports, like sea ports, are heavy polluters that foul much of their neighboring land. It therefore behooves you to distance your residential zones from your airports to lessen the negative impact on nearby land values and quality of life.

Querying Your Zones

There is a neat, little-used function in SimCity that lets you gather instant information about any area of your city. This handy feature, shown in Figure 6.4, allows you to glimpse the status of a particular land tile, telling you the kind of land, the population density, the land value, crime rate, pollution level, and growth rate.

Using the Query Function

To use the Query function, move the pointer to any part of the Edit window's map that you wish information for. Next, while pressing and holding down the *Q* key, click and hold down the mouse or joystick button (or the space bar for the PC version) and you should see the Query box pop up. Inside, important information about the current section of land is prominently displayed.

As an example, try using the Query function on a powered residential zone. If you haven't done so already, build a power plant and then establish a residential zone nearby that is electrically connected.

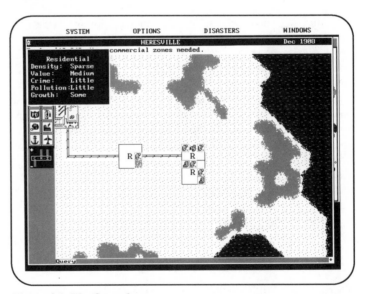

Figure 6.4: The Query box

Steps in Using the Query Function:

1. Move your pointer onto the residential zone.

2. Hold down the *Q* key and then click and hold down the space bar, mouse, or joystick button. Don't let go of the *Q* key.

3. A pop-up Query box should appear somewhere on your screen with detailed information about the tile the pointer is currently resting on.

4. Every tile has its own individual data. On the PC, you can move the pointer around the zone while continuing to hold down the *Q* key, noting the changes in the Query box. On the Macintosh, you must also continue to hold down the *Q* key, but you must release the mouse button, reposition the pointer, and then click and hold down the mouse button again before you can query another tile.

You will notice that in residential zones, the Query function will generate different readings from different tiles in the same zone. This can be useful in determining negative as well as positive influences on your zone. For example, if you find in a single zone that tiles facing a road are lower in value than tiles facing a waterfront, you will know that the road is having a negative impact on one side of your zone.

Step 7

Managing Your Money

Taxing Thoughts

To make the model more realistic, SimCity includes the effects of taxation and governmental spending on the economy. The taxes you levy on the Sims allow you to fund city services and build city infrastructure. If you manage your finances well, your revenues will increase at approximately the same rate as the demand for new zones and services. Mismanaging your funds, on the other hand, will cause a negative cash flow that ultimately results in bankrupting the city treasury.

Tax revenues are figured according to a formula that depends on the population, land value, tax rate, and a special scaling factor that changes with the game. You have no direct control over land values, population, or the scaling factor, but you can modify the tax rate up or down. It is a mistaken assumption to think that raising taxes is the best way to increase your city income. Temporarily this may work, but in the long run you may have unintended consequences that hurt your economy. The higher the tax rate, the more Sims leave your city, and the more industry and commerce is driven out, eroding your tax base and forcing down land values. With too low a tax rate you don't generate enough cash flow to maintain existing city services and allow for new infrastructure growth. The tax rate formula is a little recursive in this way, in that your tax rate affects changes that themselves affect the tax rate.

The following is the formula by which SimCity calculates Tax Revenue:

Tax Revenue = Population ✕ Land Value ✕ Tax Rate ✕ Scaling Factor

Every January, unless you have toggled on **Auto-Budget** under the Options menu, you are presented with a new proposed budget, which appears in the Budget window. In this window (shown in Figure 7.1) you must set the property tax rate and decide how much

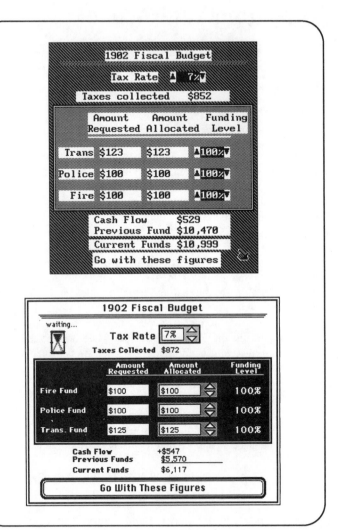

Figure 7.1: The Budget window for the PC (top) and the Mac (bottom)

money to allocate for the Transportation Department, the Police Department, and the Fire Department. When you are satisfied with your choices, click on the **Go with these figures** button to return to the game. Of course, you may at any time call up the Budget window from the Windows menu and make adjustments as you deem necessary. The money is not collected until the year has passed, so you can change your budget retroactively for the current year all the way up to December.

Gramm-Rudman Budgets

If you dilly-dally too long wrangling over the budget, the Budget window will disappear and SimCity will impose the same budget you had last year. Insufficient funds will cause SimCity to slash spending, starting with the Police Department, then the Fire Department, and finally the Transportation Department. This is essentially the same thing that happens when Congress lollygags over the budget and the across-the-board budget-cutting provisions of the Gramm-Rudman Deficit Reduction Act automatically take effect.

Macintosh users can procrastinate a little longer by clicking on the hour glass icon that appears in the Budget window. Clicking on this icon causes the sand in the hour glass to be refilled as if the hour glass were starting over again. If you note the progress of the falling sand and how empty the upper chamber of the hour glass is, it will give you an idea of how much time you have remaining.

Set Your Tax Rate

Setting your tax rate is one of the most important and powerful ways that you can control the simulator. Your efforts here are critical to the success or failure of your city, so be aware of the consequences of your actions. Taxes can be set from 0 to 20 percent in 1-percent increments/decrements. Setting taxes between 0 and 6 percent will attract new Sims, industry, and commerce to SimCity thereby furthering your tax base. The smaller the tax, the larger the growth rate.

Tax rates from 7 to 9 percent cause city growth to slow, or increase at a rather sluggish rate, but allow you to accumulate money for building. Tax rates above 9 percent are suicidal: you may initially derive some benefit from increased collections but you will end up driving the Sims away. Just below the **Tax Rate** indicator is the **Taxes Collected** indicator which tells you the amount of tax money you have taken in for the previous year.

In the Budget window next to the **Tax Rate** indicator are two arrows, one pointing up and the other pointing down. For this example, start up the **Dullsville** scenario by using the **Load Scenario** command from the System menu (File menu on the Macintosh). Then follow these steps to learn how to change the current tax rate:

1. Open the Budget window by selecting the **Budget** option from the Windows menu.

2. Increase the tax rate to 20 percent by clicking repeatedly on the up arrow in the **Tax Rate** indicator. You should see the percentage change in the text box.

3. Decrease the tax rate to 1 percent by clicking repeatedly on the down arrow in the **Tax Rate** indicator. The text box should now show 1 percent.

4. Click on the **Go with these figures** button to exit the Budget window and return to the simulator.

Don't set the tax rate at 0 percent; it severely increases crime. Setting it at 1 percent will give you most of the advantages of 0 percent, but will avoid an escalating crime problem that is associated with a rapid influx of new SimCity residents.

Establishing Funding Levels for City Services

Three columns of budget information are displayed in the Budget window. The **Amount Requested** column tells you how much funding each city department is requesting for the current fiscal year. The **Amount Allocated** column displays the dollar amount that you are budgeting for each department. You change this amount by clicking on the up or down arrows to the right of the column. (In the PC version they are on either side of the third column.) The third column, **Funding Level**, displays the amount you are allocating as a percentage of the amount requested.

Keyboard users on the PC can use the + and − keys to cycle the pointer through all the hot spots in the Budget window and then increment or decrement in steps of 1 percent by pressing the space bar or the Insert key on the numeric keypad when the pointer is on one of the arrows.

Keyboard users

You can also change the percentage amount in steps of 10 percent by clicking the right mouse button or the Delete key on the numeric keypad.

Effects of Adequate and Inadequate Funding

Transportation Department

Funding the Transportation Department at 100 percent of the amount requested will keep all the roads, rails, tunnels, and bridges in good working order. Yearly maintenance costs for roads are $1 for each section of road and $4 for each section of bridge. Maintaining your rail transit costs $4 for each rail section and $10 for each section of underwater tunnel. Underfunding the Transportation Department causes both roads and rails to start deteriorating. At funding levels between 90 and 99 percent, an occasional road or rail section will fall into disrepair, causing an interruption in service. In the Edit window, the bad portion of track or road (which could be a pothole or track problem) will look like rubble, and must be bulldozed and rebuilt in order to restore unimpeded traffic flow. Funding between 75 and 90 percent causes a more rapid decay of the transit system. Funding below 75 percent may cause such a serious breakdown that your transportation network may become disrupted entirely.

If you don't have enough money to completely fund all city services, SimCity will prioritize your budget by first allocating money for the Transportation Department, then the Fire Department, and finally the Police Department, if there is money left over.

Police Department

Each police station that you build costs $100 to maintain each year. Cutting the amount of funds that are earmarked for police results in reduced coverage of services for each station. Crime rates will then go up, as will citizen complaints, eventually leading to an exodus of residents. If you don't have enough funds to maintain all city services at the levels recommended, SimCity will first try to cut your Police Department funding before reducing funds for other departments.

Fire Department

Every fire station also costs $100 per year to maintain. Reducing funding will cause fire coverage areas to diminish in range and quality of service. This means that a fire that ordinarily would be snuffed out quickly might burn for years, destroying much property and disrupting power and transportation links. If you decide to cut back on fire services, you are gambling that the money you save will offset the increased fire risks and damage that might result. Running out of funds to pay for city services causes SimCity to first reduce Police Department funding before attempting to curtail Fire Department spending. There is a trick to save money by reducing spending for fire stations without repercussions—see Step 13.

Watch Your Cash Flow

One of the easiest indicators of how well your city is doing is to look at your yearly cash flow. If you have a positive cash flow, your city is collecting more taxes than it is spending on yearly maintenance for city services. This is the most desirable situation for you to be in because you will be building up your treasury while sustaining all vital city services. In effect you are "paying as you go." Your cash flow, whether negative or positive for the year, is shown in the Budget window's **Cash Flow** indicator, and is added together with your carryover funds from the previous year (**Previous Funds**) to give you your current balance in the **Current Funds** indicator.

The **Cash Flow** indicator in your Budget window is calculated according to the following formula:

**Cash Flow = Taxes Collected − Total Funds Allocated
for City Services**

There's Only One Golden Rule in Life:
Those Who Have the Gold, Rule

If you let your finances get out of hand, you may quickly find yourself on a downward spiral, where your income doesn't cover the cost of maintaining city services, and you have no money left over to do anything. Unless you take steps to reverse the drain on your treasury, you may end up being thrown out of office. Cut back on all spending and bulldoze all unnecessary roads and rails to reduce the financial strain. As long as you have enough money in the bank to deal with any contingencies, you will continue to rule.

Every Sneak Will Plunder If He Dare

Because the makers of SimCity saw the need to allow unconventional means of financing your city, they provided some sneaky ways of bringing in some extra cash. These methods are not without their price, for if you become too greedy, SimCity will punish you.

Embezzlement

SimCity has a built-in embezzlement function that allows you to steal $10,000 at a time. This money is added to your current funds allowing you to escape the financial restraints that bind you in a conventional game. You do this on the PC or Macintosh by typing **FUND** while holding down the Shift key. (You should be in the Edit window when you try this.) In the PC version, you cannot embezzle if you have more than $79,999 in your current funds. (There is no such upper limit with the Macintosh version.) Be forewarned, however—using the embezzlement function more than three times in a game will cause a massive earthquake to strike your city. See Step 13 to find out how to sidestep this problem. On some versions of SimCity, you are not restricted to using the embezzlement function three times; you can use it as much as you like without fear of earthquakes.

Banzai Taxation

Banzai taxation, so called for the sudden and massive tax increase that you spring upon your constituents, is the most famous of all financing schemes for SimCity. In order to understand how it works, you must remember that taxes are collected *retroactively,* once a year, the following January. Through an odd quirk in the program, you can wait until the end of December to massively raise your taxes and the program will not care that you waited until the last moment to do so. If you then lower the taxes to a modest level in January, the program will never know that you raised and collected taxes at an absurdly high level in the previous year. The Banzai taxation technique can then be repeated indefinitely. To illustrate this, if your taxes were at 1 percent for the entire year, and you decided that you needed more money, you could raise taxes to 20 percent in December and collect them the next month, in January, as if you had been collecting them at the 20 percent rate since January of the previous year. Yet in the meantime you will not have suffered the negative consequences of high taxation, since SimCity will have been fooled into thinking that your tax rate was only 1 percent for the whole year. The taxes you collect at 20 percent will be for the entire past year, even though you only raised them at the last minute in December. If you then lower the taxes back to 1 percent, you will have completed the Banzai cycle and brought yourself full circle to the tax rate you had before. Some later versions of SimCity give you citizen complaints about high taxes, so you may not have complete success with this technique.

Here are the steps to follow for Banzai taxation:

1. Wait until you are in the month of December in the Edit window.

2. Call up the Budget window.

3. Raise the tax rate to 20 percent by clicking repeatedly on the up arrow in the Budget window.

4. Click on the **Go with these figures** button to return to the Edit window.

5. Make sure **Auto-Budget** is toggled off, then wait until January's budget pops up on the screen.

6. In the Budget window, note how much more you have collected in the **Taxes Collected** indicator.

7. Lower taxes to 1 percent by clicking on the down arrow in the Budget window. (Lowering to 0 percent is not recommended because it increases crime.)

8. Laugh all the way to the bank.

Step 8
Surveying Your Domain (Interpreting Maps)

In this step you will learn how to use and interpret your various city maps as viewed in the Maps window. You will also learn how to print out a map of your city. The Maps window allows you to select one of nine icons to call up and display a map mode depicting some aspect of your city. The map modes give you different overviews of your city and provide detailed cartographic information about population, zone types, power distribution, transportation links, traffic, pollution, crime, land values, and city services. Additionally, for the PC version of SimCity, there are character markers that display the current position of important moving objects such as the ship, airplane, train, helicopter, monster, and tornado.

In the title bar at the top of the Maps window you will see the name of the particular map view you are currently looking at. At the top left hand side of the title bar you will find the familiar close button or box that you click on to close the window. Just below this you will find the icon palette containing all the Map icons used to select different map views. If you have selected a view that shows density, rate of growth, or other comparative levels, you will see a *density key* below the icon palette, on the bottom left corner of the Maps window. The main map portion of the window gives you an overview of your entire city; inside this you will see the moveable selection rectangle showing the present location of the Edit window. As mentioned before, repositioning the rectangle causes the Edit window to scroll quickly to a new position on the map.

Double-clicking on the selection rectangle for the Macintosh version of SimCity will bring you immediately back into the Edit window.

For all the examples in this step, you will need to have the **Dullsville** scenario loaded. Load the scenario now, and when it has started up, activate the Maps window by clicking on any visible portion of the window. Players who prefer keyboard shortcuts can press ⌘-*M* on the Macintosh or *Ctrl-M* on the PC (the Enter key will also work for the PC) to activate the Maps window. The Maps window for the Dullsville scenario is pictured in Figure 8.1.

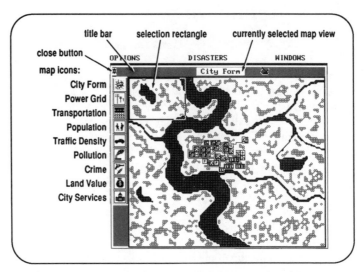

Figure 8.1: The Maps window for the Dullsville scenario on the PC

How to Display the Different Map Modes

Each map mode is activated by selecting an icon from the icon palette on the left side of the Maps window. Some of the icons enable you to select additional maps to display. For instance, if you select the Population icon (fourth icon down from the top), you will see a submenu pop up giving you the choice of displaying either the Population Density map or the Population Growth map.

Selecting Icons from the Palette

To demonstrate how you go about selecting an icon to display a particular map view, try selecting the Population icon (resembling two people standing up) by moving the pointer onto it and clicking with either the space bar (PC), mouse, or joystick button so that it becomes highlighted. On the PC, you can use the + and − keys on the numeric keypad to cycle you through all the icon choices. On the submenu that pops up, click on the **Population Density** option. A colored map will appear in your Maps window, displaying the different population densities with different shades of color (or gray scales, if you have a monochrome monitor).

Understanding the Density Key

Now that you have displayed the Population Density map, you will want to understand how to read it. The density key, just below the icon palette, gives you a visual guide to what the colors represent. High is usually signified by the color red, while low is represented by the color blue. If you have a monochrome monitor, you will be handicapped in trying to figure out the density levels, because shades of gray are harder to differentiate than color changes. Typically, for gray-scale monitors, the darker the zone the higher the density will be. Looking at your map, you will see that your most densely populated zones are in the center of Dullsville, and your lower-density zones are in the outskirts of town. Figure 8.2 illustrates the density key in greater detail.

How to Scroll the Selection Rectangle

The flashing selection rectangle, as described in Step 5, is used to reposition the Edit window. You can reposition it anywhere in your Maps window by clicking and dragging. On the PC, you can use the space bar and cursor keys to move the rectangle pointer, or you can use the mouse or joystick to click and drag.

With the Mac you need to click and drag the selection rectangle to its new position in the Maps window. With the PC, however, you can simply move the hand pointer to the desired portion of the window and then click—the rectangle will immediately move to the location of the pointer.

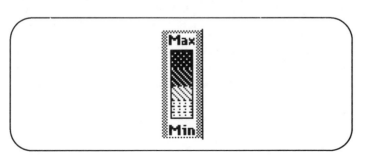

Figure 8.2: The density key

Using the Different Map Modes

The different map modes give you vital information on trouble spots around your city, allowing you to detect and correct problems as they occur. Each map focuses on a particular topic and you must therefore select the appropriate icon to display the kind of information that you are looking for. The next sections describe all your available map views and give you some insights on how you would interpret and use the cartographic data that is presented.

City Form Map (PC) and City Map: Comprehensive (Macintosh)

The City Form map on the PC shows your entire city limits, and is useful for planning where you want to place your residential, commercial, and industrial zones. If you have become disoriented or have forgotten the location of a disaster, you can quickly find it by looking in this Map view. For example, fires can be seen as little red squares, a tornado can be spotted by the letter *T,* and the Monster by the letter *M.*

Use the City Form map before you build so that you can plan where and what to build. By glancing at this map, you can also determine whether you have the correct mix of residential, commercial and industrial zones. A general rule of thumb is that the number of residential zones should equal the sum of your commercial and industrial zones.

Similarly, the Macintosh version's City Map icon shows the location of the residential, commercial, and industrial zones within the entire city limits. You have a choice with this version, however: when you choose the City Map icon, a submenu will pop up that permits you to display **All Zones,** or just the **Residential Zones, Commercial Zones**, or **Industrial Zones** separately.

Power Grid Map

A map of your entire power grid is presented if you select this option. Use this chart to quickly locate power outages and breaks in the power lines. This is especially handy after disasters but it is also helpful just for checking to see if your entire city is "plugged in." Unpowered zones contain black dots in their center, while powered zones have yellow or light-colored dots in their center. Power lines are visible by their gray lines with light-colored dots evenly spaced. To restore power, you must return to the Edit window and fix the power line breaks.

Transportation Map

All your roads and rails are clearly outlined in this map. This map is useful for planning future road or rail expansion and for showing how extensive your existing transportation network is. For color PCs, roads appear in a dark blue while rails have a lighter purplish color. If you use this map in conjunction with the Traffic Density map, you can devote attention to clearing up traffic bottlenecks and creating new access routes for your SimCitizens.

Population Map

Selecting the Population icon causes a submenu to pop up giving you two map options to pick from: the **Population Density View**, and the **Population Growth View**.

Population Density View

This map view shows you where the most populated zones are in your city. The density key tells you what color or shade of gray the different density levels are. For users with color systems, densely populated areas are displayed in shades of red, while more sparsely populated areas appear as shades of blue. Use this map to keep track of where your center of population is.

Population Growth View

If you would like to know where the areas of highest population growth are, select the Population Growth map. In this map, you can see the areas where the Sims are flocking into your city in the greatest numbers, and what areas they are fleeing from. Unlike the other maps, the density key here depicts positive rates of growth with the color blue, and negative rates of growth with the color red. Knowing the location of high growth areas in your city can be very helpful in planning where to locate new city services such as police and fire stations. Encouraging people to move into your city also becomes easier since you can build more residential zones in the highest growth areas, attracting even more new residents.

Traffic Density Map

When you start getting complaints about traffic jams, you will know that it is time to look at your Traffic Density map. Selecting the Traffic Density icon will bring up this map, allowing you to quickly ascertain where the worst congestion is located. By consulting the density key, you can spot major blockages by their red color, and roads that are relatively free-flowing by their blue color. Your next step will be to bulldoze the offending traffic arterials and replace them with rails. Don't be tempted to build wider roads, it doesn't work. Traffic will always expand to fill existing capacity.

Pollution Index Map

Since land values, particularly residential zones, are adversely affected by pollution, you will want to find out where the worst pollution is occurring in your city. Selecting the Pollution Index icon brings up the Pollution Index map, showing you the zones with the highest concentrations of pollutants. With the density key as your guide, you can see that the areas with maximum pollution levels appear red, while the areas with minimum pollution appear blue. Notice that industrial zones, sea ports, airports, and roads (but not rails) are all sources of pollution.

There are a few things you can do to help alleviate conditions in some of the more polluted areas. Relocating heavy industry away from residential zones, planting parks, and restricting new industrial development can help somewhat. Another effective tactic is to spread industry out, so that pollution is diffused more widely at lower densities. Replacing roads with rails can also help matters some.

Crime Rate Map

By clicking on the Crime Rate icon, you will be able to view high crime areas in your city. This is very useful in pinpointing locations that need more police protection. If you use this map tool as a supplement to the Police Protection map (available via the City Services icon), you can quickly and efficiently direct your police resources to curb the crime problem. High crime areas, as indicated on the density key, appear in red, while low crime areas are shown in blue.

Land Value Map

Selecting the Land Value icon summons the Land Value map into your Maps window. Use the density key to figure out which areas of the map are of higher or lower value. Because land values figure importantly in generating tax revenues, you will want to know where the high rent districts are in relation to the slums. Although in the real world redlining (discriminating economically against certain neighborhoods considered poor risks) is illegal, in SimCity you can redline all the low-life districts you want. By abstaining from placing new investments of zones and buildings for the lower-valued land, and directing your resources to the higher-valued land, you can significantly improve your tax base. If you are so inclined, you can attempt to upgrade poorer areas by building parks and increasing police protection, or you can try urban renewal by bulldozing down the blighted areas and rebuilding (see also *Urban Renewal* in Step 13).

Industrial zones and zones with high crime or pollution are predisposed towards lower land values. Most waterfront areas, you should note, tend to have a high land valuation.

City Services Map

Clicking on the City Services icon will cause a submenu to pop up offering you two choices, **Police** or **Fire**. The **Police** option will bring up the Police Protection map and the **Fire** option will bring up the Fire Protection map.

Police Protection Map

In this map, all your police stations' coverage areas are clearly delineated through multicolored squares that radiate out in all directions. The level of crime prevention falls off as the distance from the station increases. This can be seen as the squares surrounding the station appear more blue the further they are from the station. Closer in, where police protection is stronger, the squares are red, indicating a high level of crime deterrence. The density key is helpful in showing you the level of police service.

Used in combination with the Crime Rate map, the Police Protection map can guide you in the best placement for your next police station. You want to maximize your coverage and avoid useless duplication of service, so try not to have two police stations overlap their radius of coverage. Remember that each station must be properly funded, have electrical power, and adequate transportation access in order to have an optimum radius of coverage.

Fire Protection Map

Similar to the Police Protection map, the Fire Protection map shows your fire stations' coverage areas. The density key tells you whether adjacent zones have a high or low level of Fire Department coverage according to what color or shade of gray the zone appears as. The red zones surrounding each station indicate a high level of fire suppression services, while the blue, more distant zones show a weaker fire fighting ability. In order to have maximum fire prevention service, each fire station must have proper funding, electrical power, and good transportation links to get to any fires (it doesn't matter whether they are roads or rails).

The Fire Protection map aids you in deciding the location for new fire stations. When you are concerned about fire prevention but don't want to unnecessarily duplicate or overlap existing covered areas, simply call up this map and look for areas that are without coverage. Then build your station in this strategically located area to maximize firefighting efficiency.

Markers for Moving Objects (PC Version Only)

As mentioned previously, SimCity for the PC has moving markers in the Maps window to indicate the positions of moving objects (not available on the Macintosh). These markers are represented on the map by the first character of each moving object's name, as listed below and illustrated in Figure 8.3.

Marker	Object
A	Airplane
H	Helicopter
M	Monster
R	Railroad Train
S	Ship
T	Tornado

Printing

Depending on which version of SimCity you have, you may be able to print a one-page city map or a six-page poster-size map of the Edit window. This section will describe printing your map with the PC and Macintosh versions of SimCity.

Special Note on Non-Epson Printers

PC versions of SimCity will only work with the IBM ProPrinter or Epson MX, RX, FX, or compatible printers hooked up to your parallel port. (Technically, you can also redirect output from your parallel port to your serial port using the DOS command **MODE LPT1:=COM1**.) Unfortunately, because SimCity does not work with PostScript or non-Epson compatible laser printers, it won't work with the popular Hewlett-Packard LaserJet series. Fortunately there are two shareware alternatives to sidestep this problem. The first program, MAP.ZIP, reads your city file and prints it on your HP

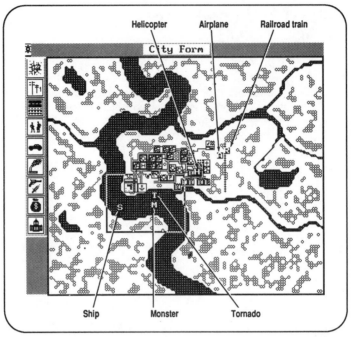

Figure 8.3: The moving object markers in the Maps window (PC only)

LaserJet or other PCL (HP's Printer Control Language) compatible printer. The second program, called EMUL8.EXE, allows your HP LaserJet or PCL compatible printer to emulate an Epson printer, thereby allowing you to print from within SimCity.

MAP.ZIP, written by Edward Greenberg of San Jose, California, allows you to print a one-page map of any city file from the DOS prompt on your HP LaserJet or compatible printer. Its advantage over SimCity's one-page map is that it clearly shows each zone type and gives you a running tally of city statistics including the total number of zone and building types. In Steps 13 and 14, you can see some figures that were printed out using this MAP program (some of these figures were cropped to fit the page). You can find MAP.ZIP on CompuServe under the Game Forum Libraries, or on many other electronic BBS (Bulletin Board System) services. MAP.ZIP is a compressed file and must be decompressed or unarchived using a shareware utility called PKUNZIP (also available on CompuServe). There are instructions that accompany the program. MAP.ZIP is distributed as a shareware program, and the author requests a $10 registration fee to keep you informed of future updates.

Another way you can print to any HP LaserJet printer is to run the shareware utility called EMUL8.EXE, which allows your LaserJet or PCL compatible to emulate an Epson printer. This way you can print from within SimCity using the Print command and generate gorgeous six-page poster-style maps of your city.

Today, many Postscript printers can emulate HP LaserJet printers by simply throwing a switch. The Apple Personal LaserWriter NT and QMS LaserWriters, for example, offer this capability. Thus, by configuring the printer as an HP LaserJet and using either of the print utilities mentioned above, you can print beautiful SimCity maps.

Printing on the PC

When you select the **Print** option under the System menu, you summon a dialog box that gives you the choice of printing out an eight-page poster of your city or a single-page condensed view. You may notice that in the Print dialog box SimCity only allows you to print through your LPT1 parallel port (although you can redirect this to a COM serial port using DOS's **MODE** command). Click the pointer on either the **8-page poster** or **1-page map** button and then click the **Go** button to commence printing. A progress report text box will then appear, informing you what percentage of the map has been sent to the printer. Should you decide to abort the printing process, press the Esc key. Keyboard users can move from button to button by using the grey + and − keys.

Printing on the Macintosh

The color version of SimCity (1.2c and 1.3c) allows you to print out a poster-size map of the Edit window on six pages of paper. When you select **Print...**, a dialog box pops up on the screen. An informal test showed that printing out all six pages on an Apple LaserWriter took approximately 9 minutes.

A warning is in order to those who are impatient. Printing out the poster-size map on six pages can take up to 21 minutes using an ImageWriter.

In the black-and-white version of SimCity (1.2b&w and 1.3b&w), the **Print** option opens up a dialog box in which you can choose to print a condensed view of the city map on one sheet of paper (**Print Map**) or the entire city as seen in the Edit window on six pages (**Print City**). Your printer must be an ImageWriter or PostScript-capable LaserWriter.

Step 9

Feedback and Evaluation

In order to be informed on your city's progress, you will want to keep track of trends over time and listen to your constituents' concerns. This information is presented in two windows: the Graphs window and the Evaluation window. The feedback you get in the Graphs window lets you spot interrelated problems that you wouldn't ordinarily connect together. The evaluation you receive from your SimCitizens in the Evaluation window helps you determine whether your policies are working or not. You don't want to lose touch with the people; if you do you may find yourself impeached and run out of town by a mob led by your mother.

Looking at Your Graphs Window

Unlike the topical data presented in the Maps window, the line graphs in the Graphs window reveal patterns and trends over time. By consulting this chart you can determine whether population and pollution are increasing at the same rate, for example, or whether crime rates are connected with upturns or downturns in industrial or commercial population growth. Armed with this information, you can make better planning decisions in the future.

To illustrate how the Graphs window works, let's first open up SimCity's **Dullsville** scenario. The Graphs window is opened through the Windows menu by selecting the **Graphs** menu option. From the keyboard you can do this by pressing *Ctrl-G* on the PC or ⌘-*G* on the Macintosh. Select the **Graphs** option now to open the window.

As seen in Figure 9.1, the Graphs window has eight icons on the left-hand side of the window. Clicking on an icon activates the graph display for that topic or time span. By looking at each graph line's color, you can identify which graph is being plotted: the highlight color or pattern around the activated icon matches the color or pattern of the graph line. You can display all six graphs at once. (Unfortunately, if you have a monochrome monitor, it is virtually impossible to distinguish between the different graph types.)

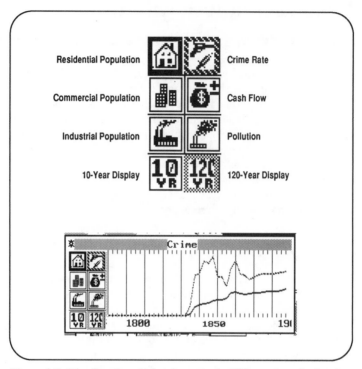

Figure 9.1: The Graphs window icons and a 120-year graph showing crime (top line) and residential population (bottom line)

Select the Residential Population graph by clicking on the house icon in the Graphs window. Around the house icon you should see a yellow highlight, and in the graphs portion of the window you should see a bright yellow line representing the total population plotted over time. Click on the **120 Year** button to see how the population has grown over the last 120 years. Notice that the graph is flat until 1835 but then moves sharply upwards, indicating that Dullsville only started to increase its population after this date. Now look at the crime rate by selecting the icon to the immediate right of the Residential Population icon. The Crime Rate icon should be highlighted in red and you should see a red graph overlaying the yellow population graph. Examining the correlation between the crime rate and population growth, you will notice that the crime rate began to skyrocket with the influx of new people to Dullsville in 1835.

What does this tell you? The more people you attract, the greater the crime problem. Therefore you must plan for increased police protection when growth in the population surges ahead.

When you are finished looking at the Graphs window, close it by clicking on the close box (close button on the Mac) located in the upper left corner of the window.

Residential Population Graph

The Residential Population graph indicates the total population for your residential zones over the past 10 or 120 years. Use this graph in combination with other graphs to discover why you are suffering declines in population. The graph appears in yellow.

Commercial Population Graph

Activating this graph will show your commercial zone population over the past 10 or 120 years. The color of the graph is black.

Industrial Population Graph

Your industrial zone population is plotted in this violet-colored graph. If you use this with the Crime and Pollution graphs, you can quicklydeterminewhenindustry began to negatively impact your city.

Crime Rate Graph

Crime increases or decreases are recorded in this graph over the time period you selected. The graph appears in red.

Cash Flow Graph

The Cash Flow graph shows you whether you have a negative or positive cash flow in your budget. Your cash flow is calculated by subtracting the cost of all city services from the revenue you collected in taxes, as figured in the Budget window. If you have a zero cash flow, you will see a straight line plotted down the middle of the Graphs window. Above the midline represents a positive cash flow, while below the midline signifies a negative cash flow. The Cash Flow graph appears brown.

The cash flow graph only represents the dollar difference between the taxes you take in and the money you spend on city services. This number should not be confused with the amount of money you spend building infrastructure and zones. Obviously the more infrastructure the more costly it is to maintain, but your cash flow has nothing to do with the **Current Funds** figure as viewed in the Budget window. Just use this graph to gauge whether or not you are spending more in the maintenance of your city than you are collecting in taxes. If you do have a negative cash flow, you must take corrective steps to stop the drain on your treasury.

Performance Evaluation in the Evaluation Window

To evaluate the results of your actions in SimCity, it is helpful to frequently call up the Evaluation window (Figure 9.2). Open up this window now by selecting the **Evaluation** option from the Windows menu. When this window opens up, you will see two sections: Public Opinion and Statistics. Interpreting the information in both sections of this window will be the goal of the next part of this chapter.

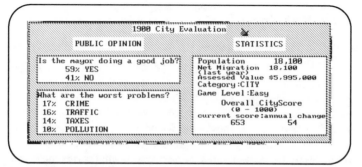

Figure 9.2: The Evaluation Window

Vox Populi: The Pulse of the City

The Sims are very vocal about what they like and dislike. In the Public Opinion section of the Evaluation window, they let you know how good a job they think you are doing and they list the worst problems that they perceive. Consulting the opinion polls on a periodic basis will let you listen to the voice of the people, allowing you to better respond to their needs.

Public Opinion

The response to the poll question *"Is the mayor doing a good job?"* is updated constantly to reflect the opinions of the Sims. You are doing a good job if you receive a Yes vote from more than 55 percent of the public. Any complaints voiced by more than 10 percent of the population in the *"What are the worst problems?"* section will negatively affect your approval rating.

Citizen Complaints

Complaints by the Sims are presented in three ways: the Public Opinion section of the Evaluation window, the message bar of the Edit window, and pop-up text boxes.

Complaints that are displayed in the Evaluation window are posed as a poll, with responses broken down by percentages, on the question, *"What are the worst problems?."* The protests are rated in descending order of importance—that is, the problem with the most votes is presented first, then the next, and so on. Generally, if 10 percent or less of your citizenry is complaining you can continue with your present course without adversely affecting your city. Anything over 15 to 20 percent will detract from your city score and cause the Sims to leave.

From time to time in the message bar of the Edit window, grumblings will surface. You can safely ignore most of the complaints that appear in the message bar if you are not concerned about your popularity. For instance, in some of the scenarios you must try to satisfy a particular "win" condition, so you probably won't care about what the citizens want. In cases such as these, you don't need to waste your time or resources bothering with trivialities. Just focus on tackling the specific problem you are trying to deal with and ignore the rest.

When a complaint message pops up in a text box, on the other hand, you had better take heed and do something quickly. Otherwise, your tenure as mayor may rapidly become history.

How to Respond to Complaints

The following section describes how to respond to the most frequent complaints that appear in the Public Opinion section of the Evaluation window. Notice that of the eight possible gripes, only the four most serious can be displayed in the Evaluation window.

Traffic

Complaints about traffic are fairly easy to deal with: just replace roads with rails. Rails will always solve your traffic problems, since they offer higher capacity and have the added benefit of lowering pollution. The Sims never complain about train noise.

Crime

Funding your police department at 100 percent and building new police stations in crime-infested areas is the way to get the Sims off your back on this complaint. Use your Police Protection map and the Crime Rate map to best determine where to place new stations. Increasing land values is another way to decrease crime.

Pollution

To stop complaints about pollution, replace roads with rails, and disperse the industrial zones to outlying areas away from your residential zones. Remove residential zones around airports, sea ports, and coal power plants, and you will get rid of the most vociferous of the whiners.

Housing

When the Sims protest about housing, they want you to zone more residential zones. This is actually an encouraging sign, because more Sims are trying to move into your city to take up all those fast-food jobs you have created.

Housing Costs

Skyrocketing land values will aggravate the Sims who are trying to find low-cost housing. Build more residential zones in low-valued land areas. Avoid zoning near waterfronts and other high-value land. Use the Land Value map and the Query function (see Step 6) to determine where your low-valued land is.

Fires

Usually, this complaint only occurs if you have fires that have been burning for a year or more. To reduce fire complaints, build more fire stations and fund them at 100 percent. If you are so inclined, you can manually intervene and bulldoze fire breaks around major blazes. This will contain them quickly.

Taxes

To stem criticism about high taxes, lower them. All tax rates 9 percent or higher will cause this complaint.

Unemployment

This problem can be dealt with by encouraging new industrial and commercial development. Zone new commercial and industrial areas and lower taxes to attract businesses.

Understanding City Statistics and City Score

In the Statistics portion of the Evaluation window, you will find yearly statistical information on the status of your city, the population, net migration, assessed value of city property, the game level, and your current score. The following section describes these statistical indicators in greater detail.

Population

Your Population count in the City Statistics section of the Evaluation window gives you the previous year's census results.

Net Migration

The Net Migration figure tells you how many new Sims moved into your city in the last year and it provides a rating system for how desirable your city is to live in. A large positive number is indicative of a healthy city, with a strong economy and plenty of good housing to accommodate the newcomers. If your net migration is negative, however, something is amiss with your city and you need to take corrective action to stem the tide.

Assessed Value

Assessed Value is the aggregate value of all your city-owned property. All improvements such as parks, roads and rails, and public works buildings such as power plants, police and fire stations, airports, and sea ports are counted in this figure. Residential, commercial, and industrial zones are not included in the assessment since they are considered privately owned.

City Categories

Although many times your goal in building a city from scratch is to see how large a population you can attract, a large population by itself does not mean your city is flourishing. You can have high crime, pollution, and other negative consequences which can make your city an undesirable place to live. The City Category classifies your city according to its population as one of six types. Table 9.1 details the city categories you can have in SimCity.

City Category	Population
Village	0 to 1,999
Town	2,000 to 9,999
City	10,000 to 49,999
Capital	50,000 to 99,999
Metropolis	100,000 to 499,999
Megalopolis	500,000 and above

Table 9.1: City Categories by Population

Score

Your score is based on a composite of major and minor factors as shown in the following list. Interestingly enough, your score does not directly depend on your population size, so a city that is small can still have a high city score as long as it has a healthy growth rate. If your goal is to have a city that stabilizes at a certain population level, however, your city score will drop because growth will have stopped.

Major Factors

Crime

Pollution

Housing Costs

Taxes

Traffic Congestion

Unemployment

Fire Protection

Unpowered Zones

City Growth Rate

Minor Factors

Stadium needed but unbuilt

Sea Port needed but unbuilt

Airport needed but unbuilt

Fully funded Transportation Department

Fully funded Police Department

Fully funded Fire Department

Uncontrolled fires

Scores can range from 0 to 1000, but average scores hover in the range of 500 to 750. Scores in the range of 550 to 800 are considered good, while scores above 800 are exceptional. If you legitimately obtain a score above 900 without cheating, you deserve a medal.

Step 10

Automating the Simulator

Customizing Features

The Options and Game Speed menus on the Macintosh and the Options menu on the PC allow you to customize the environment in which you play SimCity. Features such as **Auto-Bulldoze, Auto-Budget, Auto-Goto, Sound, Speed,** and **Animation** can be turned on or off directly from these menus. With the exception of the **Speed** and **Animation** options, your preferences are usually saved with the city file, so you don't have to reset them when reloading a previously saved city. Most of these menu commands are *toggles;* that is, they can only be switched on or off. A triangular marker symbol (for the PC) or checkmark (for the Mac) appears next to those menu options that have been turned on, with the exception of the **Sound On/Off** toggle for the PC (it appears as **Sound On** or **Sound Off**).

Using the Options Menu

Pull down the Options menu now to see the automation and customization features you have available. Figure 10.1 shows the PC and Macintosh Options menus. The **Speed** option on the PC version's Options menu pops up its own submenu. Macintosh players have a separate Game Speed pull-down menu to alter the speed characteristics of the game.

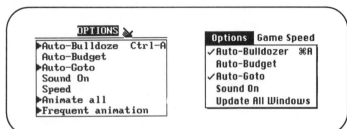

Figure 10.1: The Options menus for the PC and Macintosh

Using Auto-Bulldoze

In order to build or zone anything in SimCity, you must clear the land underneath so that it is vacant. Forests, shoreline, and other occupied land must be bulldozed before development can occur. **Auto-Bulldoze** allows SimCity to do some of this bulldozing for you, saving you the trouble of manually clearing the land yourself each time you want to use the Edit window's tool icons. For the most part, you will likely always want to keep this menu option toggled on for the convenience of not having to bulldoze the land before you build or zone. There is no advantage to enabling auto-bulldozing from the standpoint of saving money; if a land area is in need of bulldozing before building or zoning can take place, you will still be charged for the bulldozing whether you do it yourself or you let SimCity do it with **Auto-Bulldoze**.

It costs one dollar to auto-bulldoze one tile of land. Bulldozing an area of forested land can cost up to nine dollars for each residential, commercial, or industrial zone since each of those zones occupies nine tiles. Airports, sea ports, stadiums, and power plants take up more land tiles, and therefore will cost more if bulldozing is required.

Keep in mind that the auto-bulldozing function works only on natural terrain such as forests and shorelines, and a few artifices such as power lines and parks (only park tiles without a fountain). It will not work on established zones, or any other object, including roads and rails (contrary to the SimCity documentation). You must first manually bulldoze these other items before building can occur.

For the sake of demonstrating the **Auto-Bulldoze** feature, perform the following steps:

1. Open up the **Dullsville** scenario.

2. Activate the **Auto-Bulldoze** option (if it isn't on already by default).

3. Select the Roads icon in the Edit window and try building a road over some forested land. With the same icon, try to build a bridge in a straight line over some water.

4. Build some parks in a forested area using the Parks icon.

5. Select the Residential Zones icon and try zoning over your newly established parks (note that a zone cannot be placed over a park fountain).

6. Now deactivate the **Auto-Bulldoze** option, and try repeating steps 3 through 5 above. Notice that you can't build or zone without first manually bulldozing non-vacant land and you can't build or zone over water (though you can bulldoze single tiles directly adjacent to original shoreline as if you were creating landfill).

7. Reactivate **Auto-Bulldoze.**

Using Auto-Budget

Another convenience for alleviating tedium, the **Auto-Budget** option allows you to keep your budget spending priorities at the same level without pestering you for approval each year. Each year SimCity proposes a budget which you must okay or revise. Many times you already know that you will simply approve the same budget you had the year before. This is where the **Auto-Budget** option proves its usefulness. By toggling it on, you needn't concern yourself with the year-to-year approval that your budget would otherwise require. Another nice use for this option is leaving Sim-City to run for a long time unattended, such as overnight, to see how a city might evolve. Is it stable or will it fall apart? These are questions that you won't be able to answer unless you let SimCity run on for awhile.

In the event that there are not sufficient funds to meet the budget, the **Auto-Budget** option will prioritize by first allocating money for the Transportation Department, then for the Fire Department, and finally the Police Department if there is money left over.

To demonstrate how you might use the **Auto-Budget** feature, try the following example to increase your funds:

1. With the **Dullsville** scenario still open, toggle Auto-Budget on.

2. Open the Budget window and increase the tax rate to 11 percent. Next slash spending for all city services to 50 percent of the amount requested. Click the **Go with these figures** button to exit the window.

3. On the PC, highlight the **Speed** option, and in the submenu that pops up, select the **Fastest** setting. When you are done, click anywhere outside the submenu to return to the simulator. For the Macintosh, pull down the Game Speed menu and select **Fast**. This will enable time to pass more quickly while you await your January tax collections.

4. In the Edit window, watch the city date. When January rolls around, no Budget window will appear. This tells you that last year's budget was used to set this year's budget. You have now automated the Budget to always come up with the same settings.

5. To verify that auto-budgeting is still in effect, open the Budget window and you should see the same tax rate of 11 percent and city services being funded at 50 percent that you set in the previous year's budget. Exit the Budget window by clicking on the **Go with these figures** button.

6. Wait a couple of more years while you accumulate more funds before toggling off **Auto-Budget**.

7. After toggling off **Auto-Budget**, the Budget window will now reappear each January.

Using Auto-Goto

With **Auto-Goto** toggled on, SimCity will move you to the scene of a disaster or other major catastrophe so that you can sightsee before taking action. Unfortunately, you will be rudely interrupted if you were busy doing something elsewhere in the city. Should you decide to keep **Auto-Goto** off and a cataclysmic event occurs somewhere, you will hear a crash or siren noise (if the sound is switched on) and you will see a **GOTO** button and a message in the Edit window message bar informing you of the nature of the crisis. By clicking on the GOTO button (on the PC you can also press the Tab key), you will be immediately transported to the scene of the disaster.

If you are playing SimCity on the PC, pressing the Tab key after moving to the disaster will return you to where you were before the calamity occurred (or will cycle you to every location that shows that type of disaster).

Try the following example to learn how the **Auto-Goto** function works:

1. With the **Dullsville** scenario open, toggle **Auto-Goto** off (if it is already on by default) to see how the simulator functions without this feature.

2. From the Disasters pull-down menu, select the **Fire** option.

3. Soon, in the message bar of your Edit window, you should see a disaster report of a fire somewhere. Next to the message you will see a **GOTO** button. Click the **GOTO** button to instantly be transported to the scene of the crisis.

4. Return to the Options menu and toggle on the **Auto-Goto** feature. We will now compare how the simulator reacts with **Auto-Goto** enabled.

5. Again, select the **Fire** option from the Disasters menu.

6. Notice that with **Auto-Goto** enabled, you don't need to click the **GOTO** button; you are automatically moved to the problem area.

Toggling Sound Off and On

The **Sound On/Sound Off** menu option turns on and off the sounds of the city. For the vast majority of PC users with a crummy little speaker, you aren't missing much if you toggle this feature off. Macintosh users are fortunate that they have a built-in sound chip that gives a fairly good rendition of the appropriate sounds.

There are two principal advantages to keeping the sound off. First, the simulator runs a little bit faster and doesn't annoy you with its constant honking noises. Second, you can play SimCity in the office without being detected by the boss.

Setting the Speed on the PC

Setting the speed on the PC is accomplished by selecting one of the five speed options in the pop-up **Speed** submenu under the Options menu. At more complex levels of the game, you might want to speed things up as the simulator gets bogged down updating and calculating all the city's variable elements. If you are the owner of an XT or other 8086/8088 PC clone, and you do not wish to age visibly while playing the game, you might want to set the speed to the **Fastest** setting. After highlighting the speed you want in the submenu, click on it to activate the triangle marker symbol. Press the Esc key or click the pointer anywhere outside the **Speed** submenu selection box to return to the simulator. Figure 10.2 illustrates the **Speed** submenu.

Fastest

The **Fastest** setting is recommended for owners of XTs or 8086/ 8088-based PCs. However, this option may be too fast for 80386 owners. For example, a 386 running at 25 megahertz only takes about 3 seconds to update each month, or 36 seconds each year. (This is with the **Animate All** and **Frequent Animation** options toggled on.)

Actually, altering the speed of the game is a handy feature for those Simmers who like to whiz through boring years, and slow down for more interesting ones. And if you are terribly impatient about collecting taxes to pay for your pet pork-barrel project, speeding up the game allows you to accrue the money more quickly.

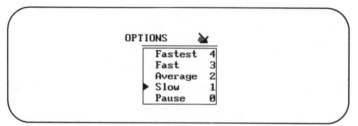

Figure 10.2: The Speed submenu for the PC

Pressing the *4* key on the main keyboard is the keyboard equivalent of selecting **Fastest**. If you want the highest performance, toggle off the **Frequent Animation, Animate All,** and **Sound,** and set game speed to **Fastest**. This will reduce the need for SimCity to manipulate the visual and aural aspects of the game.

Fast

Slightly slower than **Fastest, Fast** can be activated via the **Speed** submenu or by pressing the *3* key on the main keyboard.

Average

Average is the default speed when first starting a new or saved game or scenario in the PC version. At other times, this speed can be selected from the keyboard by pressing the *2* key.

Slow

The slowest speed option is **Slow**, and can be activated from the keyboard by pressing the *1* key. How slow is **Slow**? If you are easily irritated by delays, this is not the speed for you. On the other hand, if you are a stolid, phlegmatic couch potato, and like to agonize over every small detail, it will suit you well. The **Slow** speed is also recommended for owners of Cray XMP supercomputers, and, of course, 586 machines running at 100Mhz.

Pause

When you pick **Pause**, the simulator stops the simulator clock and with it the growth and dynamic change that your city is undergoing. You can still continue to zone and build, but none of your actions will be absorbed into the simulator's equations for calculating how quickly or slowly your city is evolving. Time is effectively stopped. This command is good for freezing the simulator so that you can go to the fridge for a snack or answer the telephone. When you come back, you won't find that you've been booted out of office as Mayor.

Setting the Speed on the Macintosh

Setting the speed on the Macintosh is accomplished through a separate Game Speed pull-down menu in the menu bar. Unlike the PC version, you have only four speed options: **Fast, Medium, Slow,** and **Pause.** Choosing a faster speed enables you to speed things up when the simulator gets bogged down updating and calculating all the myriad elements that make up the system. Click on the menu to pull it down and then select the speed you desire. A checkmark should immediately appear next to your selection indicating that the speed has been adjusted. Figure 10.3 demonstrates the selection of the **Fast** speed setting.

Fast

Mac 512 and Mac Plus owners will find this the ideal setting at more complex levels of the game, because the simulator will tend to slow down due to an overload of calculations. This speed might be too fast for newer Macintoshes, such as the Mac IIsi, which only takes about 6 to 8 seconds to update each month (72 to 96 seconds per game year). Altering the speed of the game is also recommended as a way to collect your taxes quickly, should you be short on funds.

Medium

The default speed setting when starting a new game or scenario is **Medium.** This speed option is about three times slower than **Fast.** Previously saved cities will revert to the speed they were saved

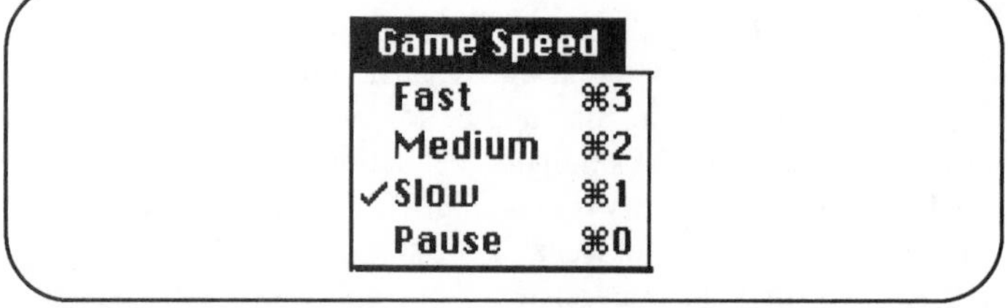

```
╭─────────────────────────────────────╮
│         ┌────────────────┐          │
│         │ Game Speed     │          │
│         ├────────────────┤          │
│         │   Fast    ⌘3   │          │
│         │   Medium  ⌘2   │          │
│         │ ✓ Slow    ⌘1   │          │
│         │   Pause   ⌘0   │          │
│         └────────────────┘          │
╰─────────────────────────────────────╯
```

Figure 10.3: The Game Speed menu for the Macintosh

under, so loading a city that was saved under the **Fast** setting, for example, will cause that city to be opened at the **Fast** speed.

Slow

The slowest speed option is **Slow**, which is about seven times slower than **Fast**. If you are easily irritated by delays, this is not the speed for you.

Pause

With this option, you stop the simulator's clock and with it the growth and dynamic change that your city is undergoing. You can still continue to zone and build, but none of your actions will be absorbed into the simulator's equations for calculating how quickly or slowly your city is evolving. Time is effectively stopped. This command is good for freezing the simulator so that you can go to the fridge for a snack or answer the telephone. When you come back, you won't find that you've been booted out of office as Mayor.

Animate All (PC Only)

The **Animate All** option, when toggled on, allows animation and updating of all windows that show motion (moving traffic, trains, ships, tornados, etc.). If toggled off, **Animate All** will animate only the frontmost window; consequently, the simulator will run a bit faster since it won't have to calculate as many moving objects. You cannot save this setting with a city file that you save to disk. It must be reset every time you load a city.

Frequent Animation (PC Only)

Refers to the amount of screen updating that will occur for animated screens. If you turn this feature off, SimCity will speed along even more quickly, since valuable CPU time will not be wasted drawing and redrawing the screens so frequently. Again, you cannot save this toggle setting to a city file, but must reset it every time you load a city.

Step 11

Dealing with Disasters

How to Create a Disaster

Natural and unnatural disasters can be set loose on SimCity through the options available under the Disasters menu. By selecting a particular disaster from this menu, you can have a fire, flood, air crash, monster, or tornado strike your city, with the potential for wreaking havoc and utter mayhem. Your city can be laid to waste, being reduced to ruins if you do not take immediate corrective action. In addition to the calamities available through the Disasters menu, there are two other disasters that can befall SimCity: shipwrecks and nuclear power plant meltdowns. These latter accidents are random events that you have no control over, so it is very difficult to prepare or defend against them. Figure 11.1 shows the Disasters menu for the PC.

Using the Disaster Menu to Start a Fire

To demonstrate how you create a disaster, first open up the **Bern, Switzerland 1965-Traffic** Scenario. Next, select the **Fire** option under the Disasters menu. Somewhere in Bern, a fire will ignite. If you have **Auto-Goto** enabled, a fire warning will appear in the message bar of the Edit window and you will be instantly transported to

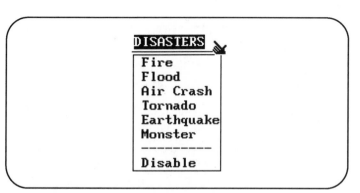

Figure 11.1: The Disasters menu on the PC

the scene of the blaze. Otherwise, click the **GOTO** button in the message bar to visit the spot where the fire erupted. In the Edit window you should see a flickering red flame tile indicating where the fire is burning.

How to Battle the Blaze

There are several strategies for containing a fire. For one thing, you can build a fire station nearby so that its effective radius of coverage overlaps the fire(s). To see the fire station's radius of coverage, select the icon resembling a city hall (the City Services icon) in the Maps window, and then click on the **Fire Protection** option in the submenu that pops up. Any fires inside the coverage area will soon be extinguished, provided that there is power supplied to the fire station, that there is road or rail access, and that you have allocated sufficient funding for the Fire Department. The station's effectiveness is directly proportional to the distance to the blaze and the funding levels you have established.

Another way you can attempt to control a fire is by bulldozing fire breaks around the fire thereby preventing it from spreading. Fires cannot cross clear land or water, but can propagate rapidly through forests and buildings, and less rapidly over roadways, transit lines, and power lines. If you surround the fire with bulldozed or clear terrain, the fire will burn itself out and stop spreading. You cannot bulldoze a fire directly.

To illustrate the bulldozing technique for fighting fires, follow the next few steps to extinguish the fire you created above in the **Bern** scenario.

1. Select the Bulldozer icon in the Edit window.

2. Scroll to the area where the fire is burning. If it is already out, or you can't find it, create another fire.

3. Bulldoze the center tile of the zone where the fire is burning. You will notice rubble replacing the land where the zone used to exist. If there is no zone where the fire is, skip to the next step.

4. Bulldoze any roads, rails, utility lines, or adjacent zones that border the fire.

5. In a short time the fire will burn itself out.

Disabling Disasters

The last menu option, **Disable** (on the PC) or **No Disasters** (on the Macintosh), prevents only new disasters from occurring. This option does not work, however, for scenarios or files that contain preprogrammed disasters. If you don't want the disaster to happen, you must save the city file to disk and then reopen it again. Upon reopening the city, the disaster will not occur—but make sure to select **Disable** to prevent any new disasters from occurring!

Other Planned Disasters

Flood

When you select **Flood**, rivers, lakes, and coastal areas will overflow their normal shorelines, damaging buildings, utilities, and transportation links. Floods, like fires, spread and wreak destruction in their path but, unlike fires, cannot be stopped. The best course of action to combat flooding is to relocate vulnerable buildings and zones to less sensitive inland areas. When the waters recede from flooded areas, the land is left clear of any features. You can rebuild on the same terrain, of course, but doing so risks a repetition of the deluge.

Air Disaster(PC)/Air Crash(Mac)

The **Air Disaster** (**Air Crash** on the Macintosh) option will cause an airplane crash somewhere in your city (but usually near an airport). The SimCity manual erroneously states that an air crash will occur only if you have built an airport, but enabling this option without an airport will, in fact, cause an airplane to materialize out of thin air and crash. Air crashes, when they occur, cause fires to break out. Firefighting techniques such as containment and building fire stations are the only effective means of managing air disasters.

Shrewd mayors will locate airports away from populated areas and then build a fire station right next to the airport to offer immediate protection to it and the surrounding neighborhood. In this case, an ounce of prevention is worth a pound of cure.

Tornado

Selecting this disaster option will cause a tornado to sweep through your city, demolishing and crushing everything in its path. Like a juggernaut, this funnel shaped torrent of rushing air and clouds will appear out of nowhere, randomly moving about and leaving a devastated city in its wake. You can't really stop a tornado from destroying property, but by following its path, you can battle any blazes it starts. This will help you to minimize any collateral damage.

As mentioned before, the PC version of SimCity uses tornados as a form of "divine retribution"—if you bulldoze a church, a tornado will appear as punishment. Bulldozing them down makes sense if you wish to revitalize the area by rezoning it so that something more productive will flourish. Many Sim-Mayors tire of having a glut of churches and hospitals occupying prime real estate and paying no taxes (thanks to their tax-exempt nonprofit status). They see these types of establishments as parasitical, scavenging valuable land and contributing nothing. Just be sure to select **Disable** before getting rid of them—unless you enjoy dodging tornados. See Step 13 for other avoidance techniques.

Earthquake

If you want to try your hand at rebuilding a city from the bottom up, try the **Earthquake** disaster option. Earthquakes, measuring between 8.0 and 9.0 on the Richter scale, are the most catastrophic disaster in SimCity and are capable of reducing entire cities to rubble. When an earthquake strikes, the landscape in the Edit window will shake and shudder, giving you a glimpse of the havoc going on below. Fires will usually break out in the aftermath of an earthquake, causing even greater devastation than the shaking itself. In fact, it was the fires after the great 1906 San Francisco earthquake that did the most damage to the city. (Some cynical historians have suggested that the fires were deliberately set by people intent on collecting insurance money, which they could not otherwise legitimately claim since their policies covered only fires, not earthquakes.) Your job after the earthquake is to put out the fires and restore power to the city. Try to contain the larger fires first, bulldozing fire breaks around the conflagration and reconnecting downed power lines to nearby fire stations.

SimCity's built-in "embezzlement" function (holding Shift while typing **FUND** in the Edit window—discussed in Step 7) allows you to steal $10,000 at a time. If you get too greedy and "borrow" more than three to five times, an avenging earthquake will strike your city down, even if you have disabled all disasters. There is no such thing as a free lunch.

Monster

Selecting the Monster disaster causes a scaly red or green reptilian creature to slither out of the water and into your city, destroying everything in its path. You must put out the fires it starts, repair the utility lines and transportation links that it demolishes, and undo the damage it causes when trains, ships, helicopters, and planes crash. Like a tornado, a monster cannot be stopped, but its damage can be minimized by scurrying after it and cleaning up the mess it leaves behind.

In Macintosh versions 1.2c and 1.3c, when the monster has been sighted, the enigmatic message shown in Figure 11.2 may pop up. Trivia fans will be delighted to learn that the Japanese writing is just a joke. The monster was created in honor of Godzilla, a heroic monster of 1950s Japanese science-fiction movies and comics. At the same time a Japanese comic-book hero named Ultraman would work with his crack Ultraman Squad to save people from monsters and other sordid characters. The advice offered in the message box

> A large reptilian creature has been spotted in the water. It seems to be attracted to areas of high pollution.
> There is a trail of destruction wherever it goes. As a last resort, try calling ウルトラ警備隊.
> Other than that wait till he leaves then rebuild from the rubble.
>
> [Click to Continue]

Figure 11.2: Especially useful advice in the Mac color versions

translates to "Try calling the Ultraman Rescue Squad." This is really meant to jape at the helplessness of your situation, because no matter what you do, there is no rescue squad to come and save you from your predicament.

The monster can also appear if you have extremely high levels of pollution. Too much pollution arouses the monster from his hibernation and enrages him. It is interesting to note the symbolism involved. In the 1950s, Japanese science fiction often used the theme of technology gone amuck, with the resultant dire consequences being world annihilation. The monsters that were unleashed by this fearsome atomic technology would attempt to destroy the very same technology that created them. SimCity's monster, then, is a creature both of destruction and salvation. He responds to the ravages of pollution by trying to obliterate industry, thus restoring the natural balance of nature.

Typically the monster will move towards highly polluted areas in an effort to snuff out the offending polluters. Although he loves to chomp on industry, the monster's favorite delicacy is airport and seaport sauté.

Unplanned Disasters

Shipwreck

Shipwrecks cause fires when the ships crash into a bridge or shore, but they can only happen if you have first developed and powered a sea port. SimCity does not take into account any damage to the environment, unlike real world accidents, so you can easily rebuild what is destroyed.

Nuclear Power Plant Meltdown

Meltdowns occur only if you have built a nuclear power plant. There is no way to cause a nuclear disaster from the Disasters menu, but if you are in a hurry to see one, you can load the **Boston 2010, Nuclear Meltdown** scenario. When a nuclear power plant explodes, fires erupt around the plant and in the adjoining land area. Many parts of the city adjacent to the plant become uninhabitable because the power plant's central containment dome will have been breached, spewing out lethal doses of radioactive particles and gamma rays. The Chernobyl nuclear disaster will seem like a picnic compared to the damage you will have to recover from. Unlike fires, radioactive zones do not just eventually disappear, but remain for a thousand years, poisoning the land and rendering it inhospitable for human habitation. Once a zone shows the radioactive symbol, it is unusable for the rest of the game (unless you have the patience to wait one thousand Sim years).

The rate at which nuclear power plants fail depends on the Game Play Level you have chosen for your city. In general, at the **Easy** level, nuclear power plants never experience a meltdown. At the **Medium** level, nuclear power plants will last approximately 600 years, and at the **Hard** level, they will only last 150 years. Of course there is an element of randomness to these numbers that makes it risky to assume that the life span of a power plant will be exactly 600 or 150 years. Think of these numbers as being a mean or average that will give you a range of values for which you can plan. What do these figures really mean to you as Mayor? The answer to this question depends on how long you plan to keep your city going. For most cities that you build, the risk of a China SimDrome happening is very small. If you plan to run your city for only 30 years or so, the risk is negligible. The SimCity model for nuclear power risks is not entirely realistic with the way the odds for an accident are calculated. Nonetheless, the elements of randomness and danger highlight the hazards of nuclear power.

There is a sneaky way to undo radiation damage: using *Terrain Editor for SimCity,* a separate program (available from Maxis) that allows you to customize your landform. Clear the radioactive symbols and reform the land using the tool icons in the Terrain Editor, save the newly edited city, and then resume your game in SimCity.

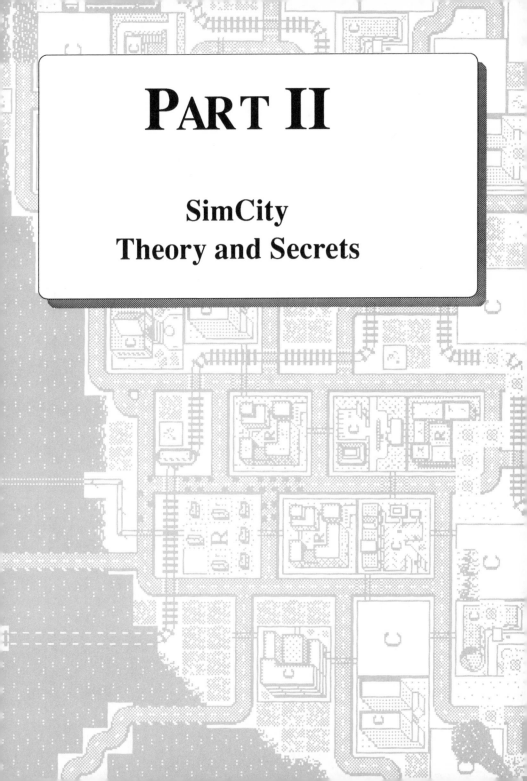

PART II

SimCity
Theory and Secrets

Step 12

SimCity's Own Agenda

This step will familiarize you with the behind-the-scenes workings of SimCity so that you may better master the subtleties of the game. SimCity is governed by a set of fixed rules that establish the working parameters of the game. You can, of course, play without needing to know these rules. But if you spend a few minutes to learn them, you will become a more cunning planner and will be better equipped to overcome any obstacles to your agenda.

The program uses algorithms to calculate such factors as population growth, pollution, crime, tax revenues, land values, internal and external markets, and traffic levels. Each of these factors affects and is affected by other factors, and the value of a certain variable changes over time as the program recycles variables that have been previously calculated back into formulas to obtain new values for the variables. To illustrate this point, land-value variables for each tile of land are affected by crime variables. Crime variables themselves are affected by land-value variables. When land value goes down, crime goes up. When crime goes up, land value is forced down even lower.

All variables are directly and indirectly affected by your actions in zoning and building. It is your job to bring all the factors together in a positive confluence so that your city may thrive and prosper. Internal factors that you have some influence over include zones, population, internal commercial markets, tax rates, city services, electrical power generation and transmission, transportation, pollution, crime, and land value. External factors that you have no control over include the external market economy (based on industrial exports outside your city) and the timing and location of disasters.

Zones

There are three primary zone types in SimCity: residential, commercial, and industrial. For your city to prosper and grow, you must establish all three types so that the Sims have a solid foundation upon which to build a productive city. The zone you establish does not contain any buildings or people when you first place it. It merely represents the grading of the land and improvements (water and sewage) so that people can start building. As such, it represents future potential and does not by itself have any intrinsic value. Value is added when industry, commerce, or Sims move in. Your goal is to attract businesses and people to fulfill the potential of the zones you build.

The Sims are important to you for three reasons: they form the backbone of your work force for commerce and industry, they pay property taxes, and they vote. The Sims live in residential zones where they build houses, condos, and apartment buildings. When the need arises, they will also build churches and hospitals that hog the whole residential zone and displace the tenants who lived there.

Factories, warehouses, and other manufacturing enterprises are found in industrial zones. These zones are economically vital to sustain growth in your city and provide needed jobs for the Sims. The manufactured goods that are produced in these zones are sold "outside" the city and bring back new money and taxes, which can then be reinvested in new industry. Early on in your city's development, these zones are crucial to building up an export-based economy to serve SimCity's external market (discussed in the next section).

The so-called "service" sector of your economy is situated in your commercial zones. These zones include retail stores, gas stations, supermarkets, banks, and offices. The commercial zones are important for their contribution to SimCity's internal market because they produce services and goods that are only consumed within your city.

Population

There are three kinds of population in SimCity: residential, industrial, and commercial. The number of jobs available in your city is represented by the industrial and commercial population numbers. Unfortunately, there is no way to take a direct reading of the commercial and industrial populations; you can only consult the Demand indicator or glance at your zone densities to get a rough idea of whether they are growing or not. The employment rate is the ratio of the commercial and industrial population to the residential population. If the ratio is less than 1, you have too many residents and not enough jobs—i.e., unemployment. If the ratio is greater than 1, you have more jobs than residents, and you will attract immigrants to your city. The following equation displays the employment rate formula:

$$\text{Employment Rate} = \frac{\text{Commercial Population} + \text{Industrial Population}}{\text{Residential Population}}$$

Residential populations are influenced by the birth rate (always positive in SimCity), employment rate (from formula above), land value, housing costs, taxes, the quality of life as measured by crime and pollution, and the presence of a stadium. Industrial populations are primarily affected by taxes, the state of the external economy (over which you have no control), and the presence of a sea port. Commercial populations are dependent on residential and industrial populations and the development of an internal economy, but are also affected by taxes. At a certain stage, the addition of an airport helps to accelerate the growth of the commercial population. All population types must have power and adequate transportation access to other zone types; otherwise they will stagnate and never grow.

Internal and External Markets

Internal markets represent the consumption of goods and services that are produced within your city. Only after your industrial base has been established will your internal market begin to grow. In effect, industry brings new people to your city, and they consume a fair amount of what they produce. As your population grows even more, they will demand more and more internally produced services and goods. This is where your commercial zones come into play. They provide the means to serve the internal market, and are essential to further growth.

External markets are the markets outside of SimCity that you export your industrial output to. You really don't have any control over the economic conditions outside your city, and occasional external recessions are inevitable. When the external economy is in recession, your industry will appear to decay and atrophy. After a while, the external economy will rebound and your industry will thrive again. To accommodate the external market's growth, you must zone more industrial zones and, consequently, more residential zones to house any new workers.

Early on in the growth of your city, you will want to emphasize the external market by building more industrial zones. Later, when the external market is eclipsed by the growing internal market, you should start adding more commercial zones. The trick is to assemble the right ratio of commercial to industrial zones during your city's evolution. As mentioned earlier, you should always try to keep the number of residential zones equal to the number of commercial and industrial zones added together $(R=I+C)$, regardless of the ratio of commercial to industrial zones.

The goal you should aim for is to have your city make the transition from an external market economy to an internal market economy. This transition is marked by a shift away from industry to commerce, at which point your city will really take off. If you plan to rezone industry to commerce, you must do so gradually, at the right time, without too much disruption. Table 12.1 shows the ratios according to population.

Population	*Ratio of Industrial to Commercial Zones*
50,000 and less	3:1
75,000	2:1
125,000	1:1
150,000	1:2
200,000 and greater	1:3

Table 12.1: Recommended Ratio of Industrial Zones to Commercial Zones by Population

Properly managing the mix of industrial to commercial zones will cause a multiplier effect to accelerate growth even further. Taking full advantage of this multiplier can mean the difference between being stuck at a metropolis population of 200,000 or growing to a megalopolis population of 500,000 or more.

SimCity's author, Will Wright, reveals a hot tip about the relationship between the city score and external market: The growth multiplier for your external market economy really begins to build momentum when your city score is high. This means that your industrial zones will grow faster when you have a high city score. Your city score is improved by population growth in your three zone types and by high land values. Your city score will decline when you have high levels of traffic, pollution, crime, taxes, and unemployment. Obviously, you must focus on all these factors to have the city score positively affect your growth in the industrial zones.

Tax Rate

By setting the tax assessment rate in the Budget window, you directly affect growth. Raising taxes decreases your city's growth rate but increases your income. It also causes the Sims to complain and eventually to move out. Lowering taxes encourages growth and brings new Sims into your city, but reduces your income. Table 12.2 shows the effects of the various tax rates.

Tax Rate	Effect
0%-6%	Fast growth in all zones. Diminished tax revenues.
7%-9%	Slows growth. Tax revenues steady.
10%-20%	All zones decline. Population decreases. High tax revenues initially, decreasing quickly.

Table 12.2: Tax Rates and Their Effects

Changes you make in your tax rate will not have an effect until taxes are collected in January of the next year. When planning your tax strategy, remember that the ideal is to have your taxes just high enough to give you sufficient income to grow, yet not high enough to cause residents and businesses to flee your city. You can use high tax rates as a means of "braking" the economy or as a growth control measure. Reducing taxes to minimal levels will help you jump-start an ailing economy.

Power

Without power, zones cannot develop or grow. If a zone goes without power for an extended period of time, it will soon decline to an empty zone devoid of people. Disasters and accidental bulldozing can cause your power transmission network to be severed; therefore, duplication of some power lines may help prevent blackouts and keep your city growing. Avoid waiting too long to fix downed power lines. You don't want all the zones that you have painstakingly helped to grow go up in smoke. Excessively long power lines, or power lines that are unnecessarily redundant, contribute to power line inefficiencies (resistance in the line). Keep line lengths to a minimum where you can, and your power losses will be kept small.

Transportation

As stated earlier, SimCity favors rails over roads as a means of transportation. Roads, to their detriment, always fill to capacity no matter how wide you make them, and they create air pollution. Rails can carry significantly more people, and they pollute less. SimCity compensates for its rail bias by making roads cheaper to build and maintain. Although it is possible and feasible to build an entirely roadless city, using only rails, you cannot easily afford to replace all your roads with rails. As an experiment, you could even try building two mirror-image cities on opposite sides of a river, one with roads only and the other with rails only. Then observe which city does better, given equal funding and development resources.

SimCity simulates traffic flow by a method known as *trip generation*. Each zone attempts to generate a number of trips, according to its population, that terminate in a different type of zone. A trip is considered successful if it travels down a road or rail and reaches its destination zone. The origin zone, or zone where the trip started, must have road or rail access to a destination zone as shown in Table 12.3.

If no transportation links exist between the origin and destination zones, the trip will be considered a failure. Additionally, the trip is limited by a *trip range* which is significantly decreased by heavy traffic. Trips that are uncompleted due to range limitations, traffic jams, or destination zone inaccessibility, will eventually cause the Sims to abandon the origin zone. This is why when your roads have reached the traffic saturation point (you'll know when this happens because you'll get increasing complaints from the Sims), you should replace them with rails. Failure to do so will result in a decline in your zone populations.

Origin Zone	*Destination Zone*
Residential	Commercial or Industrial
Commercial	Residential or Industrial
Industrial	Residential

Table 12.3: Origins and Destinations for Trip Generation

Pollution

Pollution negatively affects your residential zones, land values, and city score. Its primary causes are industrial zones, airports, sea ports, coal power plants, traffic, fires, and damaged nuclear power plants (radioactive contamination).

Crime

The effects of low land values and increasing population densities contribute to the growth of crime. Usually when you build industry, land values will drop in the immediate vicinity and crime will blossom. As described earlier in this step, the twin influences of crime and land value feed upon each other, creating a vicious circle. The more crime you have, the more land values drop, contributing to an even greater crime problem (et cetera, ad nauseam). Although not documented in the SimCity manual, population levels are definitely hindered by crime. This may be indirectly attributable to the lowered land values engendered by the escalating crime.

Conversely, good police coverage and high land values work in tandem to bring down crime rates. Your most cost-effective tactic over the long run is to increase land values. Raising land values also has the added benefit of increasing your tax revenue. Building more police stations is the quick fix solution to crime over the short haul, but it is costly because of the yearly maintenance funding. Also, adding more and more police protection, like building more prisons, doesn't really deal with the source of the problem.

Land Value

Land value is a very understated subject in SimCity, yet it is crucial to understanding the underlying rules of the game. Land values determine whether a particular area is desirable or not, and directly affect the amount of taxes you can collect. Parks, forests, and, above all, water contribute to the value of land. In order to maintain high land values, therefore, residential and commercial zones should take advantage of these terrain features. This means you should build residential zones along waterfront land and adjacent to forests and parks before building elsewhere. SimCity also bases land value on the proximity to the "downtown" as measured by the geographical center of your commercial and residential population mass. The closer to your "downtown," the higher your land values. In areas of lower land value, you can attempt to boost land values by building parks.

Land values are also negatively influenced by pollution, crime, and the distances Sims must travel to get to work. Long trip ranges, i.e., the distance between an origin zone and a destination zone, cause the origin zone to decrease in value. This rule applies mostly to commercial and residential zones.

Step 13

Tips and Tricks

In this step you will find useful SimCity information that is not commonly known. You will also discover interesting quirks and tricks that allow you to fool the simulator and take the upper hand. If you are looking for a tip or trick for a particular aspect of the simulation, you can skip directly to the appropriate topic heading and browse through the related material.

Unfortunately, because of different implementations of SimCity, not all versions will have the same results. Most of the examples provided here were executed on a PC, so if you find that one doesn't work on your Macintosh, don't be too disappointed. I hope you find this chapter as fun as I did.

Pitfalls to Avoid

Don't raise your taxes above 9 percent. It really does you more harm than good over the long run. More Sims will move away, growth will stall, and those Sims that remain will grumble.

Build only what you need now, not what you need for the future. For example, you don't need to build an airport immediately when you start your city. Wait till a more suitable time, when you have plentiful tax revenues and commercial development. When you start a new city, you don't need to build a huge road or rail network. Build small, paying for what you can afford with your current income.

Tricks & Tips

Planning Considerations

There is an infinite number of ways to build a successful city in SimCity. A good way to start your city, though, is to start building around the high-valued waterfront areas. This allows you to take advantage of the beneficial effects that water has in boosting land values in your zones. You might want to consider the layout of your downtown before you start building. Think about where would be a good central location for your commercial districts, where your outlying residential areas should be, and how you should place your industrial zones on the outskirts of town so that you can minimize the effects of pollution. Next, figure out the best way to lay out your transportation network. One idea for doing this is to have rail lines radiating from your downtown to all the outlying communities. Roads can then serve the lower-density suburbs and industrial zone areas. This plan is but one of thousands of possible variations, so feel free to experiment. That is what SimCity is all about: it allows you to tinker with the dynamics of a living city.

One of SimCity's best aspects is its ability to function unattended. For example, you can leave the simulator running overnight on your computer, and wake up in the morning to find out how your city has evolved or changed. (To save your screen, turn off or darken your monitor.) This allows you to prototype and test to see if your city has a viable design. If your city is stable, it won't fall apart and you will have proved your planning prowess. If it is not stable, you can try again with a different design approach until you get it right.

SimCity's ability to function alone is also useful in accumulating large surpluses of funds for your budget. After leaving the simulator on all night, if you have a stable city with a positive cash flow you will wake up a rich mayor. Just be sure that you disable all disasters in the Disasters menu, set the speed to the fastest setting, and toggle **Auto-Budget** on under the Options menu. Toggling **Auto-Budget** on will save time because SimCity won't pause each January for a proposed budget, and setting the speed to a fast setting ensures that more SimYears elapse overnight. Turning disasters off is essential; otherwise you may find your city has burned to the ground while you were asleep at the switch.

Zone and Building Regeneration

Zones and buildings that have been damaged due to disasters will appear with rubble in them. If you restore power to the zone or building and bulldoze the rubble away, the zone/building can heal itself and regenerate the damaged portions. In the event the damaged zone or building has only one center tile still standing, you must resupply power to that center tile before regeneration can take place. Note that roads, rails, and power lines cannot heal themselves after being damaged, so the damaged sections must be rebuilt.

Residential Zones

Despite your best intentions, the population of SimCity tends to level off between 200,000 and 300,000 people. The key to reaching a population of 500,000 is to increase population densities and raise land values while keeping crime rates low. Passing the 500,000 mark is a sure sign that you have mastered the SimCity paradigm.

Here is one less-than-honest strategy for getting to the megalopolis level of 500,000.

1. If you have the *Terrain Editor* (a separate program) for SimCity, create a land mass that has as little water as possible. This will ensure that you have adequate land space for population growth. If you don't have the Terrain Editor, keep terraforming new land masses until you find one that has little water. You terraform new cities by selecting the **Start New City** option under the System menu (File menu on the Mac).

2. Use the Hex Edit Trick (described later in this step) to quickly accumulate $2 billion.

3. Turn off all disasters.

4. Reduce your taxes to 1 percent or 0 percent. This will encourage rapid growth.

5. Put all your industrial zones on the perimeter of the map. This will leave the heart of your city pollution-free.

6. Build a sea port, airport, and stadium. Add nuclear power plants as necessary.

7. Group your residential and commercial zones in the center of the city. Mix them to achieve diversity.

8. Build only rails to connect your zones. This will prevent traffic from becoming a pet peeve of the Sims.

9. Blanket your city with police stations, especially in the industrialized sectors, where crime tends to skyrocket due to low land values.

10. Add parks and preserve forests as much as possible to keep land values high.

11. Set the speed on the fastest setting, and be patient. Deal with any problems that crop up.

12. The city should grow if the conditions of high land value, low crime, low average traffic densities, and low pollution are met.

13. If your population is growing slowly each year, let the simulator run overnight in order to accumulate people. Before you do this, toggle on the **Auto-Budget** option under the Options menu and the **Disable** option (**No Disasters** on the Mac) option under the Disasters menu. Next set the game speed to the fastest setting. These three actions will speed up your game and prevent disasters from occurring while you are indisposed.

Some people make it their goal to see what the highest stable population is that they can achieve. "Stable" is defined as a city that is not losing money, where the citizens are content, and where there is no great fluctuation in the population count. The current record for the highest stable population is held by James Alton, whose ingenious design holds around 1,038,840 people. In Figure 13.1, you can see a zone map of Mr. Alton's city, named Mill2. This map, which takes up a full 8½ x 11-inch page, and which is reduced here to fit, was printed on an HP LaserJet using a special shareware printing utility called MAP.EXE (see Step 8 for instructions on how to obtain this program). Alton used the Terrain Editor program to pack more zones together by overlapping and reducing the sizes of the zones and buildings. Land area was increased to cover the entire map with the exception of a thin river near the edge of the residential districts. Notice that industry is situated on the perimeter of the map to minimize pollution effects on the residents. Parks and the moatlike river separate the industrial zones from the residential zones, thereby raising land values and absorbing the ill effects of pollution. Residential zones are placed in a belt between the commercial core of the city and the outer industrial zones. Rails and nuclear power plants were built instead of roads and coal plants in order to maximize the efficiency of the city's infrastructure.

Another interesting goal to try in SimCity is to see how small a population you can keep that is stable (as defined above). The lowest stable population I have heard of has been around 480 people, in a city designed by A.D. Perkins.

You can overlap residential zones to achieve higher population densities. To do this, bulldoze one side of a newly placed residential zone. (This is sometimes difficult with the Mac versions of the program.) Then place a new residential zone that overlaps the bulldozed section. You will have two zones occupying less space than they would have if they had been placed separately. (Step 6 shows an example of this in Figure 6.3.)

You can also increase densities by waiting to build new residential zones until the other residential zones have fully developed and are nearly full. This way, you force the Sims to cram into what little space you make available to them. The disadvantage of this strategy is that housing costs will be higher, because not all the Sims can afford to live in your high-priced condos.

If you are trying to keep population densities low in residential zones, you can bulldoze one corner of a residential zone and replace it with a park. Note that only residential zones that have not yet passed the "house" stage can have this done to them. (On the Mac you have to wait until a house appears; then you must bulldoze it and create a park on the same tile.) A residential zone with a park in it can never develop beyond single-family dwellings, which is the idea behind this trick. Figure 6.3 in Step 6 illustrates this with a residential zone that has been frozen at the single-family level.

Isolated residential zones that are far away from the city center will stabilize at the single-family level and will not develop further. You can help them grow a little if you group them together with at least

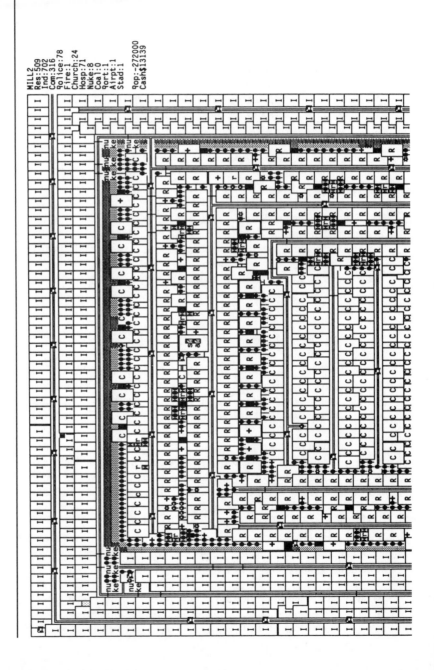

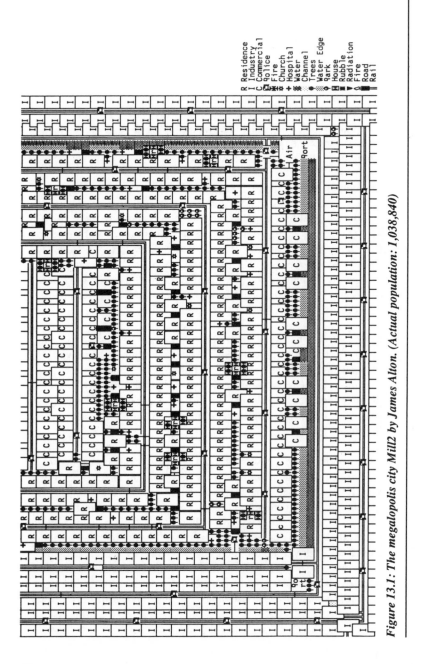

Figure 13.1: The megalopolis city Mill2 by James Alton. (Actual population: 1,038,840)

two or three other residential zones so that they share adjacent sides. The principle here is that similar zones tend to mutually assist each other.

The Urban Renewal Trick allows you to replace slummy districts with higher-value zones. All you do is plow down your decaying zones and replace them with new zones in the hope of raising land values. Sometimes it works, sometimes it doesn't. It helps to build parks that will boost land values.

Sometimes after a disaster your residential zones will be partly demolished. If you have at least one center tile remaining, the zone can be salvaged by removing the rubble and allowing the zone to heal (see above notes on how zones heal themselves). Make sure that the damaged part of the zone is not preventing the flow of power to the zone. Power is necessary for rebuilding to occur, so reroute power lines if you see a problem. Note that with only one center tile left in a damaged zone, you must build a power line to the center of the zone or else regeneration will not occur.

Churches and hospitals are often a nuisance because they can appear on valuable residential real estate that might be better suited for housing. However, when you bulldoze a church in the PC version of SimCity, a tornado sweeps down on your city to seek divine vengeance. To prevent the tornado from striking your city, select the **Disable** option on the Disasters menu before you bull-doze the church.

Once you bulldoze a church and put in a new residential zone, the church can pop right back into your new residential zone, leaving you right back where you started from. To prevent a recurrence of the church, immediately bulldoze a corner of your new residential zone and build a park. The park will keep the church away while you build a residential zone somewhere out in the boonies for the church to occupy. Churches don't care where they are situated and only come into being after SimCity has decided that a new church is needed. Unfortunately, you must keep the park in the residential zone till the rest of the seven empty squares in the zone have been built with houses. To remove the park any earlier than this risks having the church return. After the seven houses have been built, bulldoze the park to clear land. Soon, the corner will regenerate and a house will pop back in. The residential zone will now be rid of the church, and is free to evolve into apartment highrises.

Commercial Zones

As an inside joke, Maxis put its name on commercial zones that are classified as upper land value, first density level. If you have trouble identifying what the zone looks like, look it up on the Zone Evolution Card that comes with your SimCity documentation. To see the Maxis name, use the Query function on the right middle tile of this commercial zone, and you will see that the zone type is "Maxis," rather than "Commercial."

Industrial Zones

Build your industrial zones on the edge of the map. That way half the pollution will blow off the edge of the map and not impact your residential and commercial communities.

If you clump industrial zones together, you will have better development results since similar zone types develop better in groups rather than individually.

As you zone industrial zones, be sure to add lots of parks in the vicinity. Doing this will keep land values high and reduce pollution. The parks should touch the industrial zones for optimum results.

High city scores will improve the growth of your external economy. As a result, your industrial zones will grow much faster. Pay attention to the factors that influence your city score, as mentioned in the *Internal and External Markets* section of Step 12.

Pollution

Excessively high pollution levels trigger a monster attack.

Avoid having too many heavily traveled roads next to residential zones. You will hear no end of complaints over this.

Industrial zones, airports, sea ports, fires, and areas of radioactive contamination all have a "dead" zone of three to five tiles radius around them. A dead zone is an area of heavy pollution that you want to keep people away from. In general, keep your residential and commercial zones out of this area or they will develop poorly and the residents will complain to city hall about pollution. Parks and forests are a mitigating influence in reducing the size of dead zones.

Transportation

Save money by keeping your bridges and tunnels to the shortest length possible. Maintenance costs on these big-ticket items can rise quickly if you don't get in the habit of being thrifty. When deciding whether to build bridges and tunnels to islands, think about whether the zones you build there are ever going to bring in enough revenue to pay back the costs of construction and upkeep.

Traffic on roads always gets congested on curves and at intersections. Try to avoid having a road intersection right at the mouth of a bridge entrance. If you don't heed this advice, you are guaranteed to have a traffic bottleneck.

There is a built-in bias towards rails in SimCity. Use them wherever possible instead of roads. For outlying suburban residential zones, however, it is more economical to use roads because the lower population densities will not generate the traffic to justify expensive rail transit.

You can ignore some of the messages that appear in the message bar without harm. For example, when the message *"More roads required"* appears and you already have all your zones covered by either rail or road transit, this message is meaningless. Another message you can ignore is *"Inadequate rail system."* As long as each zone has some form of transportation, you can safely disregard these warnings.

Don't bother building wider roads when you have traffic jams, because traffic will always eventually expand to fill unused capacity, and you will end up with traffic jams again. Replace with rails.

Try to build zones on both sides of your road and rail thoroughfares. This is more efficient because your zones will be sharing transportation resources, instead of wastefully hogging a personal strip of road or rail.

All zones in SimCity only need to have a road or rail touch one tile in the zone for the whole zone to be completely connected. It is extravagant and unnecessary to completely encircle a zone with roads or rails.

Using the Transportation Budget Saving Trick, you can slash transportation spending to nothing and still keep your roads and rails in working order. All you need to do is build a power line over each road and rail tile. Because SimCity doesn't allow roads or rails with power lines on them to deteriorate, you can reduce the Transportation budget to zero, and not worry about your roads and rails falling into disrepair. Note that you can't build power lines along curves, bridges, intersections, and tunnels; you must still fix these segments when they go bad. To see how this looks, refer to Figure 13.2. The power line segments appear to *cross* every road and rail tile.

Another interesting trick in SimCity involves the curves, turns, and intersections of roads, rails, and power lines. In the SimCity documentation, you are told that you can only lay straight sections of roads, rails, and power lines over water. This is only partially true. Although visually this rule is correct, SimCity will still allow you to connect your rails, roads, and power lines as long as they touch sides. This means, for example, that a road can lie adjacent to another road or meet another road over water at right angles. Even though they don't look connected, they really are, and traffic will flow through the seemingly disjointed road. The same rule applies for power lines and rails. Figure 13.3 illustrates this principle in greater detail.

Police and Fire Stations

Sometimes, when using the Query function on police stations, you will get a reading of high crime! I leave it to you to ponder this one.

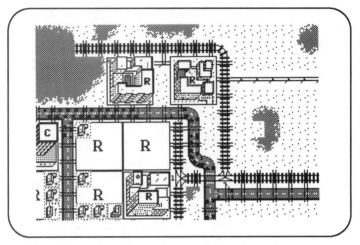

Figure 13.2: Power lines covering roads and rails to save on the transportation budget

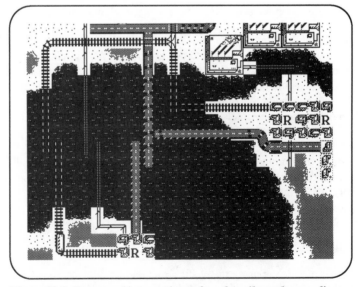

Figure 13.3: Turns and intersections of roads, rails, and power lines over water

Police and fire stations can be fooled into thinking they have complete transportation access by building one solitary road or rail tile next to the station. You save money by not having to build connecting roads or rails to the station, and you don't have to pay for their yearly upkeep. Figure 13.4 illustrates a police and fire station that are fully operational using this trick.

To maximize your police and fire stations' effectiveness avoid overlapping their coverage areas. Use your City Services map in the Maps window to strategically plot the best locations for the stations. One strategy is to keep them in a checkerboard pattern so that they cover as much ground as possible without uselessly duplicating coverage. Figure 13.5 illustrates this idea with fire stations in a checkerboard arrangement. Also, avoid placing police and fire stations on waterfronts or the edges of the map. This wastes too much of your coverage area on uninhabited territory.

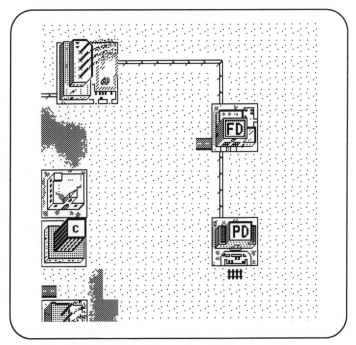

Figure 13.4: Police and fire stations transportation trick

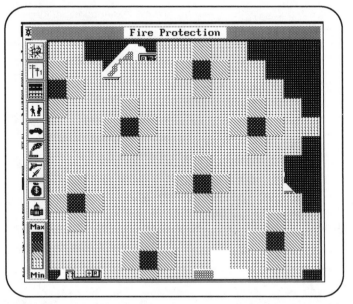

Figure 13.5: Maximizing fire coverage with a checkerboard arrangement

Crime

Most crime is generated in heavily industrialized areas. To deal with this problem, build plenty of police stations. Residential and commercial populations are more sensitive to crime and will bitterly complain if you don't do something. You can check your progress on fighting crime by using the Crime Rates map, or by consulting the opinion polls in the Evaluation window.

Building parks near industrial zones and in areas of high crime will also help reduce crime. If you situate zones near water, forests and parks, you will help minimize crime because higher land values drive crime rates down.

Avoid long rows of tightly packed zones with roads down both sides. It is better to separate blocks of zones with green space (forests and parks) in order to keep land values high and crime rates low.

Remember that high pollution, low land values, high population growth rates, and extremely low tax rates go hand in hand with high crime rates.

Airports and Sea Ports

Only one airport and sea port are needed for a city. Any more are unnecessarily redundant, and serve no purpose. SimCity does not recognize extra airports and sea ports as contributing to your commercial and industrial population growth.

A sea port can be placed anywhere on your map and, as long as there is power and transportation, it will contribute to your industrial population growth. A fun trick is to place your sea port out in the middle of the desert, hook up power, and then watch as a ship magically appears somewhere out on the water. Landlocking your sea port out in the boonies is actually a good idea—for two reasons. First, the heavy pollution it emits will blow over uninhabited land. Second, it is not occupying high-value waterfront land. Valuable waterfront land can be put to much better use by zoning residential and commercial zones, since these zone types are more sensitive to land values.

Airports are best located in corners of the map, on islands, peninsulas, or other areas with water nearby. The reason for this strategy is that if there is a crash you want to increase the odds for it occurring over uninhabited land or water where it will do little damage. This will also help limit the negative effects of pollution arising from the airport.

Because of the potential for air crashes, airports should always have a fire station constructed next to them. Fires from crashes at airports are not to be dismissed lightly. If a fire is not snuffed out quickly, your airport will burn down and you will be out the $10,000 it cost you to construct it. Don't be penny wise and pound foolish with fire stations here. Nickel-and-diming on fire protection when you have an airport isn't worth the risk.

In the early stages of your city development, you will want to emphasize industrial development and should therefore build a sea port to aid this process. Only much later, when you are moving to an internal economy based on commerce, will you want to build an airport to accelerate commercial growth.

If you are running SimCity unattended for a period of time, such as overnight, you can prevent air crashes by unplugging the airport from the utility network. Unplugging your airport has the added benefit of not causing your commercial zones to regress as much as they would if your airport were destroyed or non-existent. To unplug your airport, bulldoze the nearest power line or powered zone that connects your airport to the power supply of the city. This will disconnect your airport, temporarily ceasing all its activity. There will be no flights by your airplane or helicopter until you restore power. This trick will prevent your city from burning down while you slumber or attend to other matters.

Power Plants

Coal power plants are best situated on the corners and edges of the city map. This will help minimize the negative effects of pollution, since half the pollution will blow off the map into somebody else's backyard.

Nuclear power plants are a better choice than coal plants in SimCity because of their greater cost effectiveness and absence of pollution. At the Easy game level, a nuke has an average life span of around 600 years before failing and melting down. However, by placing your nuclear power plants in one of the four corners of your city map, you can cancel out three quarters of your risks in the event of a meltdown. To understand this, picture your nuclear power plant as having a circle surrounding it. Only a 90-degree quadrant of the circle is affected by the plant (i.e., one fourth of the circle's area), because the rest of the circle (three fourths, or 270 degrees) lies off the map where it doesn't concern you. Any damage that does occur will be limited, since three quarters of all the radiation will spew out the uninhabited ends of the map. Only the quadrant that the power plant is in will be affected.

A nifty little quirk in SimCity, called the Brownout Connection Trick, allows you to build power plants anywhere on your map without connecting them up to your power grid. This can only happen after you have built your first power plant. When you get the message, "Brownouts, build more power plants," all you have to do is build a power plant anywhere on the map; you don't have to connect it. The power plant will still pollute if it is coal burning, but can be easily placed in isolated spots where it won't bother anyone. You will save money by not having to build power lines to the distantly located plant.

Stadiums

As with other public works, SimCity doesn't care where you place stadiums. You can build a stadium on a corner of your map, far away from the city, and it will still provide all the benefits of a stadium closer to your downtown. All that is required is that you have power and one road or rail tile next to the stadium. SimCity will only check to see if there is a road or rail tile adjacent to the stadium; it does not bother to see if the road or rail goes anywhere.

If a ball game is going on in the stadium, you might want to check on the score by using the Query function on the playing field. The score is always 49ers 7, Bears 10.

Building a stadium helps your residential population grow. There is no advantage to building more than one stadium for your city; one will suffice.

Taxation and Finances

Higher land values create higher tax revenues for your treasury. This is because zones that are built near water, forests, and parks will be assessed taxes at a higher rate.

Bulldoze all non-essential roads and rails. The yearly maintenance costs for unused transportation links drains your treasury and saps your financial strength. The money you save can be applied to more productive pursuits.

The Banzai Taxation Trick can be used to fool the Sims into thinking they have low tax rates even while you are raking in maximum tax revenues. Step 7 describes this technique further.

Lowering taxes, while increasing zone populations and growth, tends to increase crime. By lowering taxes to 1 percent instead of 0 percent, you can bypass some of the crime increase.

You can save money on city services by eliminating all Fire Department funding using this simple Fire Department Trick with no fire risk to you:

1. Select **Disable** (**No Disasters** on the Mac) under the Disasters menu. From now on, no new fires will appear.

2. Reduce all Fire Department funding to zero in the Budget window.

3. Reap the financial windfall.

Another trick, known as the City Services Funding Trick, allows you to freeload money from SimCity to pay the yearly cost of your Police, Fire, and Transportation departments without your spending a nickel. This trick makes use of an unusual financial giveaway the first year you start or load your city. In SimCity, the first year of your city is considered a "grace period," in which all city services are fully funded. The Budget window will show that all budget allocations have been set to zero. In reality, however, the simulator is allocating money to all your city services at 100% of their requested funding. To take advantage of this loophole, just save your city and reload it. When you reload the city, your current year of city services will be fully funded thanks to the generosity of SimCity. You can repeat this trick as many times as you like, not paying one cent to maintain your city!

Land Values

Natural shoreline has a higher value than landfill shoreline that you create with the bulldozer. Building on landfill is thus not as advantageous as building on unspoiled waterfront land.

Proximity to water raises land values. Therefore, always build your residential and commercial zones near water before building elsewhere. Don't squander precious shoreline by building industrial zones on waterfronts. Industry is already predisposed towards low land values because of the pollution it emits. You don't need to destroy what good land you already have.

Parks and forests also raise land values. Let them remain, especially around high crime and high pollution neighborhoods. Don't bulldoze forests unnecessarily when you can avoid it.

Disasters

Flooding seems to be more invasive and bothersome in the Macintosh version of SimCity. Maxis states that a higher randomness multiplying factor for floods may cause this phenomenon.

Once you have had a nuclear accident, the land around your nuclear plant will be contaminated for at least 1000 years. Radioactive land cannot be bulldozed clear, and is unfit for any other purpose. Surrounding zones will be heavily affected by the pollution it emits, so land values will plummet and crime will rise. Short of starting your city over, you can only relocate your affected zones to safer ground or you can use the SimCity *Terrain Editor* Trick of scraping off radioactive land tiles. The Terrain Editor, a separate program from Maxis, can remove any land feature in your city, allowing you to resume your game when you have edited the city to your liking. If you have the Terrain Editor, here is how you do this:

1. Save your city and exit SimCity.

2. Start up the Terrain Editor.

3. From the System menu in the Terrain Editor, select the **Load City** option, and in the dialog box that pops up, reload your previously saved city.

4. In the Edit window, select the **DIRT** icon (top icon from the palette on the left side of the window).

5. Position the square pointer over each radioactive tile and click. Each tile will disappear to be replaced by clear land.

6. Pull down the System menu and select the **Save** option to save your city.

7. Reload your city in SimCity.

Disasters can be avoided by saving your city and then reopening it. This technique is called the Disaster Avoidance Trick. After you restart the city, you must immediately select the **Disable** option (**No Disasters** on the Mac) under the Disasters menu to prevent a recurrence of another disaster. An example of this trick is demonstrated in Step 3, but if you want to understand why this happens, refer to Step 11 for further detail. Note that previous fires or flooding will not be affected by this trick.

Fires cannot be bulldozed directly. To manually extinguish fires, you can bulldoze fire breaks and let them burn out. Make sure you bulldoze everything, including roads, rails, power lines, zones, parks, and forests. See Step 11 for proper firefighting techniques.

Helicopter and train crash disasters are very rare. Train accidents only occur when a monster or tornado runs over the moving train. Helicopters crash when an airplane intersects the path of the helicopter and they collide. To decrease the chances of this type of disaster, avoiding building congested roads around your airports. The helicopter likes to hang around heavy traffic, so having it linger around the approaches to the airport will increase the likelihood of a crash.

Cheating

There are several ways to cheat in SimCity. The most famous is the Embezzlement function. Less known, but more devious, is the Hex Edit Trick. The Embezzlement function is built into SimCity and allows you to "borrow" $10,000 at a time. You must beware of overusing this function, however, because you will be struck by a devastating earthquake if you use it more than three to five times. The actual number of times you can use this function before the earthquake strikes varies according to your version. To embezzle money on both the Macintosh and PC version of SimCity, hold down the Shift key and type **FUND**. Instantly, an additional $10,000 will be deposited to your bank account. For some earlier Macintosh versions you might have to click on the Bulldozer icon in the Edit window after holding down the Shift key or the CapsLock key and typing **FUND**.

If you are truly avaricious, there are clever little tricks to get around the above restrictions for the Embezzlement function. You can embezzle more than three to five times by employing a variation of the Disaster Avoidance Trick (discussed in the previous section) to escape the earthquake. After embezzling three times, simply save your city to disk, quit SimCity, then restart the simulator and reopen the city file. Be sure when you reopen the city to select the **Disable** option (**No Disasters** on the Macintosh) under the Disasters menu to prevent future disasters from happening. The earthquake disaster threat will be removed when you save your city, and upon restarting SimCity and reloading your city, you can begin embezzling again. If you repeat this operation, you can embezzle as much money as you like, whenever you like.

When embezzling in the PC version of SimCity, you are only allowed to accumulate up to $89,999 in your budget. When you reach this budget ceiling, you must spend at least $10,000 (i.e., so that you have $79,999 or less in your budget funds) before you can embezzle again. On the Macintosh, there is no budget ceiling for embezzlement.

Hex Editing your budget allows you to endow your city with up to $2 billion! Essentially, you change the budget data in the city file to a higher number. The data can be edited most easily when it is displayed in a hexadecimal format (i.e., base 16: where the characters 0 through 9 and A through F represent the numbers 0 through 15). On PCs, you can use DOS's *Debug* program or a disk utility program such as *Norton Utilities* or *PC Tools* to edit city files so that they contain more money than before. Macintosh players can edit the city files using *Norton Utilities for the Macintosh* or other similar utility programs. If you don't have these Macintosh disk utilities, you can always transfer your city file to a PC, edit it with DOS's *Debug,* and re-transfer it back to the Mac.

Only city files with the DOS extension .CTY or Macintosh city files can be edited. ***Do not attempt to hex edit the SimCity program itself. You will wreck the program.*** Note that the eight scenarios can only be hex edited if you first save them to disk as city files.

The following examples show you how to hex edit your city file on the PC. First you must save a city to disk giving it a name such as **Budget.CTY**. In order to run the *Debug* program, you must have your DOS directory listed in the Path statement of your autoexec.bat file, or Debug must be in the same directory as your city file. Then follow the next few steps to add $2 billion to your budget:

1. At the DOS prompt type

    ```
    DEBUG Budget.CTY
    E D24
    7F
    E D25
    FF
    W
    Q
    ```

2. Restart SimCity and load the **Budget.CTY** file. Your city will now have over $2 billion to spend.

If you are using a disk utility such as *Norton Utilities* instead of *Debug,* you will find that your funds are stored at hex C24, C25, C26, and C27. Hex locations C24 and C25 are normally filled with zeros if you started out with less than $65,535. Changing hex C24 to 7F and hex C25 to FF, as shown in Figure 13.6, will give you $2 billion.

Using DOS's redirection capabilities, you can even automate your hex editing to work with any city file, using one simple step. You must first create a text file containing the hex codes using a text editor or DOS's **COPY CON:** command. Let's try this now. Enter your SimCity directory and type the following lines at the DOS prompt.

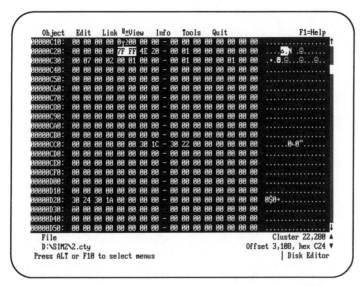

Figure 13.6: The hex locations to change if using Norton Utilities to give yourself $2 billion

```
COPY CON: SIMBANK.TXT
E D24
7F
E D25
FF
W
Q
```

Then press *Ctrl-Z*. Your text should be copied into a new text file called **SIMBANK.TXT**. Now to hex edit your city, all you need do is type the following at the DOS prompt:

```
DEBUG BUDGET.CTY<SIMBANK.TXT
```

With this technique you can add $2 billion to any city file that you substitute for Budget.CTY.

If you tire of constantly using debug to hex edit your budget, don't despair—there are shareware programs available that will quickly do the job for you. One such program, called **SIMBANK.EXE**, is available for downloading from many online BBS services.

Other Tips and Tricks

In SimCity, there is only one helicopter, one ship, one airplane, and one train regardless of how many sea ports, airports, and separate rail lines you build.

Without cheating, the real upper limit of city scores is around 900.

Using the *Terrain Editor,* you can edit your airport, sea port, or other polluting zone down to a smaller size without losing the benefits that they provide. You will have two benefits by doing this. First, you will free up more land space for building. Second, you will reduce the polluting effects of the zone to a much smaller radius. Figure 13.7 illustrates a fully functional airport and sea port that have been reduced in size through this method.

The **Pause** function under the **Speed** submenu allows you to build and bulldoze while the simulator is stopped. This is helpful for some scenarios or cities because you can freeze development while you take care of a disaster or other problem, and then speed up the simulator to collect your taxes the following January. You make better use of your time because you are not constantly distracted by other events. For example, you may have a fire that is spreading. Pausing the simulator will allow you to deal with the fire before it has a chance to do further damage. When you are finished containing the fire, speed up the simulator to collect your taxes on your next payday. Time will pass more quickly, and you won't be as frustrated waiting for the simulator to update itself.

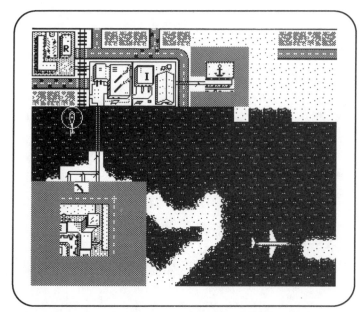

Figure 13.7: Functioning airport and sea port that have been reduced in size by the Terrain Editor

PART III

Winning Strategies for the Eight Model Scenarios

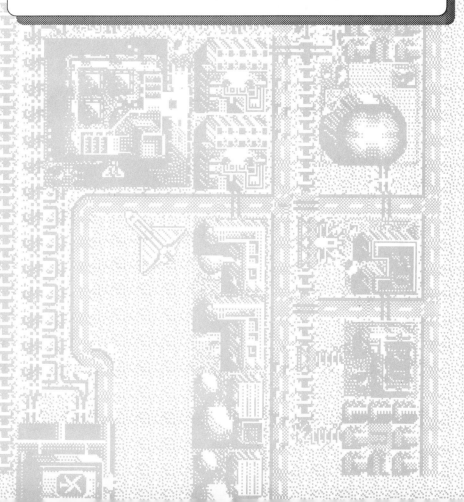

Scenario 1

Dullsville, USA 1900—Boredom

Difficulty: Extremely Difficult

Time Limit: 30 Years

Win Condition: Metropolis

Complication: Lack of Money and Time

In the Dullsville scenario, you must attempt to build a metropolis—a city of 100,000—within 30 years. This scenario tests your abilities to the utmost, for in order to meet this challenge, you must clearly understand basic theory and strategy for SimCity. You may think that Dullsville should be easy to win since the SimCity documentation states that it is "Easy." Dullsville is not "Easy," and gives even seasoned SimCity experts trouble. Don't underrate this scenario, it is by far the hardest of the eight scenarios to win.

Unlike any of the other scenarios, where you begin with $20,000, in Dullsville you only start out with $5,000 cash. Unfortunately, this puts a severe crimp on your planning since you are solely dependent on tax revenues to pay for your grandiose plans. You need to simultaneously develop your tax base and your city's infrastructure to win this scenario. This means you can't cut taxes to spur growth but must keep them high enough to raise the capital necessary for development. If your taxes are too high, you will retard growth, so you must find a happy medium. A good rule of thumb is to keep your taxes at a neutral 7 percent, which is neither too low nor too high to negatively affect your economy.

Strategy

This scenario requires you to use every available tool in SimCity's arsenal of icons. Along the way toward building your metropolis, you will need to build parks, a stadium, a sea port, and an airport. Figure 14.1 illustrates a successful Dullsville metropolis to emulate. This elegant and clever design, by James Alton of Titusville, Florida, shows you but one tack you might take in winning this wickedly difficult scenario. The Dullsville map was printed out

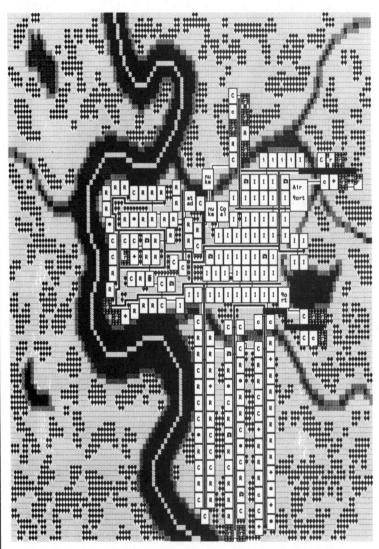

Figure 14.1: A successful Dullsville metropolis, by James Alton

with the shareware printing utility MAP.EXE described in Step 8. Because of size limitations in this book, the map from this program was reduced to fit the page. Notice the map legend which identifies all the zones, buildings and land features. Above the legend, you will see a statistical profile of Dullsville telling you the population, remaining funds, the number of residential, industrial, and commercial zones, and the number of other types of buildings.

Taking a closer look at the Dullsville map, you can see that most of the heavy industry is located east of the city, while commercial and residential districts are mostly to the south and east. The industrial zones are buffered from the residential zones by commercial zones, parks, and forests. The airport and sea port, being dirty polluters, are also placed conspicuously away from residential neighborhoods. Residential zones make use of the waterfront's ability to raise land values, and parks help improve values in the downtown area (the westernmost portion of the city). A downtown stadium attracts new people into town, thereby helping residential growth. Roads have been almost completely removed and replaced by rails, resulting in smooth traffic flow and reduced pollution. Notice also how there are only a handful of underwater tunnels, and that these tunnels are the minimum length possible. Every effort is made to avoid crossing water, saving money on the cost of expensive bridges and tunnels. This explains why development is found mainly to the south and east, rather than to the west, where you must ford an extremely wide river. Two nuclear power plants supplement the original coal power plant that Dullsville inherits when you start the scenario.

Pause the Simulator The main trick to winning Dullsville is to always pause the simulator after each new budget is approved. You only have 30 years to elevate your city to metropolis status, so every second counts. The idea here is that when you pause the simulator, you aren't frittering away precious time while you decide what needs to be done. Building and zoning should also be accomplished while the simulator is paused. When you run out of money for the current year, select the fastest speed to hasten the collection of taxes for next year's budget.

Turn Off Disasters The last thing you want to worry about in this scenario is disasters. Do yourself a favor and toggle off disasters in the Disasters menu. The scenario is frustrating enough without the additional aggravation of being wiped out by an earthquake or dealing with fires. Also, you will save money by not having to build or fund any fire stations.

Replace Roads with Rails Immediately bulldoze your traffic-plagued road network and replace it with a modern, convenient light rail system. Traffic woes will disappear and pollution levels will drop. Just be sure not to build any costly underwater tunnels except where you absolutely need them. Where you do build tunnels, keep the lengths short to keep maintenance costs down. Don't cross the river to the west; you cannot afford it with the time and money limitations of this scenario.

Keep Taxes at 7 Percent Although you may at times be tempted to lower taxes to encourage rampant growth, don't. You will reduce your primary source of income for building new zones and buildings in Dullsville. Any taxes higher than 7 percent and you might as well kiss the game goodbye.

Build a Stadium Downtown In the *first year*, you need to build a stadium to accelerate population growth. Build it in the centrally located downtown area for easy access by the Sims. Make sure that the stadium is electrically connected and that it has transportation access.

Build a Nuclear Power Plant When you first start Dullsville, you already have 30 buildings and zones that obtain their power from a single coal power plant. The coal plant can only supply power for 50 zones, but you can only support around 44 zones before brownouts occur (due to line losses and other factors). Realistically, then, you have electrical capacity for only 14 more zones. Plan now to save the $5000 you need to build a nuclear power plant. Even though the cost is more than it is for a coal plant, nuclear plants give you more value because they cover more zones than coal plants per dollar spent. Also, you can place them anywhere suitable on your map, since they don't emit pollution. By the 7th year of the scenario, you should construct a nuclear power plant to supplement the coal power plant. Later, around the 20th to 25th year of the scenario, you will need a second power plant.

Build Residential and Commercial Zones South of Downtown
You will need to start expanding your city in a different direction where there is plenty of vacant land. Of course you could consider the west part of the map across the river, but that would be impractical, for two reasons. First, you would have to build and maintain expensive transportation and utility links, and second, your new districts would be too far from your job-producing industrial zones. If you consider expanding east, you will run into your industrial zones and you will be plagued by pollution complaints. The best solution is to start expanding south, where there is a small river to cross and plenty of low-cost land.

Start by building a straight rail corridor down through the south of Dullsville. Build residential and commercial zones on both sides of the rail to maximize efficient transportation access. This is probably the best way to plan rail lines since two zones can share each segment of rail, as seen in Figure 14.1. Don't make the mistake of having to build rail lines on opposite sides of your zones. Dual rail access is wasteful and unnecessary since only one tile on a single zone side needs to touch a rail for complete zone coverage.

Commercial zones are also good insulators for keeping pollution away from residential zones. You can see this in Figure 14.1, where commercial zones partition Dullsville's residential districts from the heavy industrial district to the east. Mix the residential zones with the commercial zones to achieve a well-blended environment that will create many *trip generations* (see Step 12 for definition). The more trips, the more prosperous the zones will be.

Place Industry East of Dullsville   Start building new industrial zones east of downtown. This will keep industry close enough for residential and commercial districts to thrive, yet far enough away so that pollution does not heavily impact them. Don't build industry in the downtown or southern part of Dullsville. Industry should be kept physically apart from residential and commercial districts. Notice that the ratio of industrial to commercial zones in Figure 14.1 favors industrial zones. This is as it should be. Early on in the evolution of your city, you need to emphasize industry so that you can build up a strong export-driven external market.

Commercial/Industrial Zone Ratios   You should build 20 percent more industrial zones than commercial zones to prod the external export market into expanding. Therefore for every six industrial zones, you should build five commercial zones. Commercial zones do well in busy downtown areas, where they are accessible to both industrial and residential populations.

Build Police Stations in Industrial Areas   Crime will fester in industrial areas without police protection. Plan the best placement of new police stations to bring crime levels down. Too much crime will slow growth, so don't ignore this problem. In Figure 14.2, you can see that Dullsville ended up with nine police stations, four of which are in the eastern industrial district. You will definitely need to place a police station in the southern residential/commercial district.

Situate New Residential Zones along the Waterfront   Around the 10th or 11th year, build up your downtown area by building new waterfront residential zones. In the center of the downtown, build some commercial zones to give the residents employment opportunities and places to shop. This will keep land values high and help increase tax revenues. Build rail and power lines so that each residential and commercial zone is connected to your transportation and power network. Each zone needs only one tile touching a rail, so don't waste money encircling zones.

Build a Sea Port   Around the 12th or 13th year of the scenario you must build a sea port to further accelerate the growth of industry. If you haven't the funds, start saving now by holding off on other construction projects.

Save Money to Build an Airport   If all goes well with your city, you will need an airport to advance the fortunes of your commercial zones. The airport's $10,000 cost is prohibitively expensive, yet you must have it for population to top the magic 100,000 person count. Start saving early in the game for this big-ticket item, which you probably won't need until 22 to 26 years into your game.

Charting Your Progress in Dullsville Table 14.1 gives you an idea of how Dullsville progressed to the metropolis pictured in Figure 14.1. It lists the number of Dullsville's zones and building types, the population count, and funds left over after key years. You can use this table as a guide to chart your own game's progress. For example, if you compare the 11th year of your game with the year 1910 in the table, you will see that this version had at that point 35 residential zones, 16 industrial zones, and 18 commercial zones, with a total population of 34,600 people.

The Best Laid Plans of Mice and Men Despite your best intentions, you may find that no matter what you do, your economy just doesn't grow. This is reflected by your demand indicators, which dip into the negative portion of the graph. What you are experiencing is a recession, where your external market is slumping and the demand for your exports is declining. If this happens, you might as well throw in the towel and start the Dullsville scenario over. There just isn't enough time to weather this downturn in the economy (unless you want to try cheating—see below).

Year Ending	1900	1902	1906	1910	1928
Residential Zones	17	20	21	35	79
Industrial Zones	11	12	12	16	57
Commercial Zones	9	9	11	18	45
Total R, C, & I Zones	37	41	44	69	181
Ratio: I/C Zones	1.22	1.33	1.09	0.88	1.26
Police Stations	1	2	2	4	9
Fire Stations	1	1	1	1	1
Churches	1	1	1	2	8
Hospitals	1	1	1	3	9
Stadium	1	1	1	1	1
Power Plants: Nuke	0	0	1	1	2
Power Plants: Coal	1	1	1	1	1
Sea Ports	0	0	0	0	1
Airports	0	0	0	0	1
Funds Remaining	$372	$97	$10	$68	$815
Population Count	19,400	20,340	27,520	34,600	102,420
Major Projects Accomplished	Stadium	New Police Station	Nuclear Power Plant	Two New Police Stations	Sea Port, Airport, 5 New Police Stations

Table 14.1: Statistical Profile for a Winning Dullsville Scenario

Alternative Strategy: Embezzle Funds (Voodoo Economics) If you are unable to win with the above strategy, you might consider embezzling funds to finance your economic miracle. I like to call this voodoo economics, because there are parallels to the supply-side economic policy of the 1980s in the United States. The basic strategy is, cut taxes to zero, borrow money to pay for government services, and allow unfettered economic growth to take care of all problems. In SimCity, all you need to do is embezzle money using the tricks outlined in Step 13, slash the tax rate to zero, and build along the same lines as the first strategy of this step. Using this alternative strategy, you are free to devote your attention to planning and building your city without the worry of running out of money.

San Francisco, CA 1906— 8.0 Earthquake

Difficulty: Moderately Difficult

Time Limit: 5 Years

Win Condition: Metropolis

Complication: Earthquake

This scenario recreates the devastation from the great 1906 San Francisco earthquake and the resulting fires, which took an even higher toll in lives lost and property destroyed. In many cases, whole blocks of houses that survived the earthquake were dynamited down to clear fire breaks. In the San Francisco scenario, you are primarily concerned with reducing fire damage and clearing away rubble after the earthquake hits. The scenario starts in January, 1906, and since the earthquake will strike in April, 1906, you have only three months to prepare. However, with the **Pause** feature enabled, you can take all the time you need to plan your defense.

Strategy

The strategy to win this scenario is pretty straightforward. Before the earthquake strikes, you must pause the simulator to give yourself time to prepare. During the pause, you should build fire stations throughout San Francisco to suppress fires. To ensure reliable power distribution, you should duplicate power lines, especially between fire stations and power plants. This added power line redundancy will help keep your fire stations functioning after the earthquake. Next, you should build an airport south of the city while you still have the funds, to later encourage commercial development.

Upon completing the above preparatory tasks, you should set the speed to slow, and allow the earthquake to happen. The Edit window map will shudder and shake, simulating the effect of an earthquake. Immediately after, you will see fires erupt and explosions occur. At this point, you need to contain the fires and perform restoration work. If all goes well within the five-year time limit, your residents will return and you will have won the San Francisco scenario.

The following sections outline the main objectives you need to accomplish in order to win the scenario.

Pause the Simulator   As mentioned earlier, you need to pause the simulator to give yourself time to make earthquake preparations. After the opening screen you should quickly select **Pause** from the Speed submenu (Game Speed menu on the Mac). Do not waste time before performing this step—you only have three Sim-months before the earthquake hits in April.

Disable Disasters   Once you have paused your game, you should disable other disasters that might impair your ability to deal with the earthquake. Disabling disasters through the Disasters menu will not stop the earthquake, but it will prevent tornados, monsters, air crashes, and floods from occurring. Fires will still break out as a result of the earthquake, but you won't have to deal with random fires ignited by pyromaniacs. With disasters disabled, you will also be able to bulldoze churches without bringing the wrath of God down upon you.

Build an Airport   While the simulator is still paused, take time out to build an airport in southeast San Francisco. Building an airport, even if it is historically inaccurate for the scenario, will enhance your economic base and help your city recover from the quake. With an airport, commercial growth will zoom ahead after the earthquake, thereby encouraging the residents to move back into town. A good location would be near the bay next to the two adjoining coal power plants. Make sure you connect the airport with power and transportation access to make it fully functional.

Build More Fire Stations   One thing you should immediately notice about the San Francisco scenario is that there are only two fire stations for the whole city. Compounding this lack of fire protection, the two stations that do exist have overlapping coverage areas, thus uselessly covering the same area twice.

Obviously, you need to build more fire stations. The question is, where do you build them in congested areas where there is no empty land to place them? The answer is simple. Wherever you see a hospital or church, bulldoze it and replace it with a fire station.

Using the Fire Protection map, try to create a checkerboard arrangement of fire stations to completely blanket the city. Note that since you should have already disabled disasters under the Disasters menu, bulldozing a church will not cause any retaliatory tornados to appear.

Preventive Medicine Now that you have built your fire stations, you should check that they have road or rail access, and that they have power. A really good way to protect yourself after the earthquake is to build duplicate power lines from each power plant to each fire station. Doing this will ensure that your fire stations will have electricity, and will continue to provide good coverage after the earthquake. In times of emergency, it is helpful to have a duplicate power feeder line. Lay one out across the width of San Francisco through Golden Gate Park in an east-west direction. Another power line might travel in a north-south direction, connecting up with the Golden Gate feeder, and going south on into South San Francisco. When the earthquake strikes and you lose power to many districts, you can "plug" the duplicate lines into the nearest power plant to quickly reestablish electrical service. Without the feeder lines, you will waste too much time finding and repairing the broken connections that are causing the blackouts. You can see the power line layout as single lines in Figure 15.1. (You can also see the locations of the fire stations.)

Set Speed to Slow Once you have finished with your preparations, set the speed to **Slow**, and let the earthquake happen. The Edit window will begin to shake violently, telling you that you are experiencing the earthquake.

After the Earthquake, Pause the Simulator After the trembling subsides, pause the simulator so that you can take stock of your situation. Find out where the big blazes are, and where power outages are most acute. Fire stations, you should remember, take priority over all other zones, so you should investigate whether they have power and road access. Resume your game only when you have satisfied yourself that there is nothing more you can do.

Control the Fires Using fire-fighting techniques learned earlier, bulldoze fire breaks around fires. Make sure that no object, except

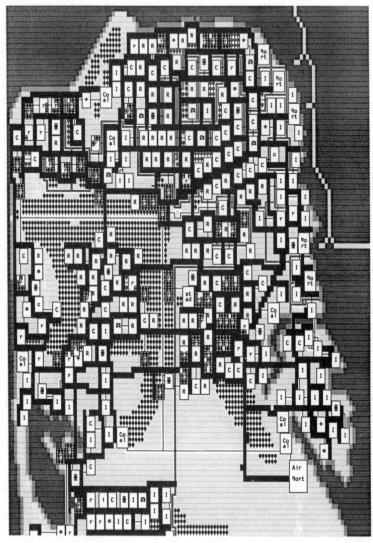

SF
Res:139
Ind:60
Com:52
Police:8
Fire:15
Church:6
Hosp:6
Nuke:0
Coal:7
Port:5
Airpt:1
Stad:1

Pop:107740
Cash$2260

R Residence
I Industry
C Commercial
□ Police
▓ Fire
⊕ Church
✛ Hospital
▒ Water
▦ Channel
♣ Trees
▒ Water Edge
♦ Park
⌂ House
▦ Rubble
▼ Radiation
▮ Fire
▯ Road
▌ Rail

Figure 15.1: One possible approach to preparing for the earthquake

rubble, touches a side or even a corner of a fire tile. If you don't bulldoze a complete fire break, the fire will spread to zones, rails, roads, power lines, and buildings.

Clear Rubble   After containing the bigger fires, start work on eliminating the rubble in damaged zones, roads, rails, power lines, and buildings. You have to bulldoze the rubble tiles that are inside damaged zones or buildings, or else they will not be able to regenerate themselves. This healing process is crucial to your winning the scenario.

Restore Power   With **Pause** enabled, you can't really see which zones are powered or not, since the flashing power symbols will not flash. To see them, you will need to resume the game, so go ahead and set the speed to **Slow**. Try to restore power to all districts that have lost power, using your Power Grid map as a guide. Be on the alert for power lines that connect to damaged portions of zones and buildings. Zones or buildings will not be powered until the power line touches an undamaged portion of the zone or building.

Rebuild and Renew   Proceed with your plans for rebuilding and renewing the city. If all goes according to plan, within five years you should win the San Francisco scenario.

Scenario 3

Hamburg, Germany 1944—Fire

Difficulty: Easy

Time Limit: 5 Years

Win Condition: Metropolis

Complication: Fire Storm from Bombing Attack

The Hamburg scenario places you in the middle of wartime Germany of 1944. You will be the target of an Allied incendiary attack on your city, and you must act quickly to put out the fires and minimize the collateral damage wrought by the bombing. When you start the scenario, you will have only a few moments before the bombing begins. The scenario starts you out in January of 1944, and when the bombing is finished it will be April of 1944. You may still experience explosions after this time, but they are the result of zones or buildings exploding from out-of-control fires, not because of any additional bomb detonations.

Strategy

Your assigned goal in the Hamburg scenario is to return Hamburg to its metropolis population of over 100,000 within five years of the initial attack in 1944. The moment Hamburg is bombed, the residents will start to move out. At first, only a few people will leave, but as the extent of the fires and damage increases, it soon hemorrhages into a rout. You must find a way to stop the exodus, in order to sustain the city's metropolis population level and win the game.

Like the other scenarios, you will make use of the **Pause** feature, so that you have ample time to prepare for the bombing. At this point, you should also disable disasters so that you may later mow down churches with impunity. The last thing you want is a church on fire that you cannot touch because you are afraid of a tornado. To save money on maintenance, you will want to bulldoze all the superfluous railroad tracks on the deserted west side of the city. Your next stratagem will be to build plenty of fire stations to smother any fires that are started by the bombs. In areas that are densely populated, you can bulldoze a church or hospital and replace it with a fire station. After you have done this, you will set the simulator's speed to slow and let the bombing take place. The bombing raid will begin almost immediately, and you can either pause after each explosion to deal with individual fires, or you can pause after the attack has finished to get a better overall damage assessment. While you are paused this second time, you can bulldoze zones and buildings that are on fire, bulldoze rubble in damaged zones and buildings, establish fire breaks, and reconnect severed power lines. Once the fires are out, you should concentrate on rebuilding Hamburg to attract back the residents who left.

Pause the Simulator Brook no delay, pause the simulator immediately! When you start the Hamburg scenario, you have only seconds before the bombing begins. If you fidget too long and the bombing starts, you must start the scenario over.

Ignore Messages in Message Bar You may notice the message, "Commerce requires an airport," in the message bar. Don't bother responding to this message or any other. Your primary concern is surviving the bombing attack and rebuilding Hamburg. Building an airport will drain your treasury and contribute little to your reconstruction efforts.

Disable Disasters The primary motivation for disabling disasters is that you can then bulldoze as many churches as you want without the worry of a tornado appearing. Quite often you will need to bulldoze a church, either because it is on fire or because you need the land for a fire station. Disabling disasters will not prevent the bomb attack or the resulting fires, but it will prevent disasters such as flooding or earthquakes from happening.

Get Rid of Unnecessary Tracks on the West Side To save money on track maintenance, bulldoze all unnecessary railroad tracks in the south and west side of Hamburg. There are quite a few tracks that have no zones or buildings adjacent to them. Particularly wasteful are the numerous underwater subway crossings, which are very expensive to maintain, and which are hardly ever used. Since you have no use for these tracks, get rid of them. Where there is duplication of service to a zone, either by rail or road, trim away the excess transportation fat so that you can balance your budget. Because of the negative effect of the bombing on the economy, Hamburg tends to have a negative cash flow. Keep trying to save money wherever you can, and your cash flow will eventually improve.

Build a Road to Your Stadium The Sims need transportation access to your stadium, which initially has no road or rail service. Therefore, connect a road to the stadium from the nearby road network. The stadium will help the economy to improve once the disaster has passed.

Build More Fire Stations If you look at the Fire Protection map in the Maps window you will see that Hamburg has only one fire station for the whole city (Figure 16.1). This is obviously an unacceptable situation to be in, considering what is about to happen. You should construct new fire stations to thoroughly cover the entire city, as well as the uninhabited forest land within city limits. Forests

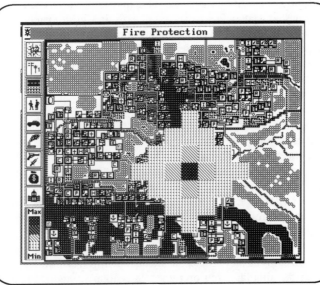

Figure 16.1: Only one fire station for Hamburg before the bombing

are at risk for catching fire should bombs fall in them, so placing one or two fire stations in their midst will help snuff out such fires before they spread in all directions to neighboring zones. Remember that for full coverage, fire stations must have power and be connected with transportation.

If you are environmentally conscious and want to preserve your forests, you may object to bulldozing down trees to make way for roads to connect your fire station(s). To save the trees, you can use the Police & Fire Departments Transportation Trick demonstrated in Step 13 and build only a single road tile next to each station, fooling the simulator into thinking it has complete transportation access. New fire stations should be spaced far enough apart that they cover the entire city yet don't overlap coverage areas. Unfortunately, some neighborhoods have no room for a new fire station. In this situation, find a nearby church, hospital, or vacant zone and bulldoze it to make way for the fire station.

Set Speed to Slow   After completing your preparations, set the simulator's speed to **Slow**. The bombing attack will begin in a few moments. You will hear and see the explosions where each bomb detonates, and you will see the fires that result. Unfortunately, every bomb blast takes time to sound off on your speaker, thus slowing the attack down to a crawl. I prefer not to listen to percussive noise, and therefore always turn the sound off for this scenario. Furthermore, once you've heard one bomb blast, you've heard them all, because they are all identical.

Pause the Simulator after Each Bomb Blast   If you want to deal with each bomb blast on an individual basis, you can pause the simulator after a bomb explodes. Then you can bulldoze the afflicted zones or buildings and create impenetrable fire breaks. When you are satisfied that you have successfully contained the bomb damage, you can set the speed to slow and wait for the next bomb explosion. Repeat this procedure of stopping and starting the simulator for all the other bombs to come.

Of course, if you prefer to let the attack finish, you can wait it out by letting the simulator run on rather than stopping and starting for each bomb explosion. The benefit of this tactic is that you can work more effectively with an overview of the totality of the situation than you can with numerous partial views of local conditions. Also, you will get through the game more quickly.

Bulldoze Bombed Zones or Buildings   A zone or building that has been bombed usually erupts in flames. The best way to put out the fires and prevent them from spreading is to bulldoze the rest of the zone or building directly. Therefore, the general rule to follow is *If a zone or building is burning, bulldoze it.* Sometimes the fires will be extinguished immediately; other times they will burn on for a while, eventually dying out.

Control Fires   Using the techniques presented in earlier chapters, create fire breaks and bulldoze clear any potential combustibles. If you are successful in extinguishing all fires, you can reduce funding for your Fire Department to 0 percent to save money.

Bulldoze Rubble   To allow healing of zones and buildings that are damaged, you must bulldoze the rubble that appears inside them. If power and transportation links are functional, the zones or buildings will regenerate themselves.

Reconnect Power Lines   Carefully reconstruct your power line network so that power is restored to the entire city. All zones will need to have power for you to win this scenario.

Rebuild and Renew   Rebuild new zones and buildings to replace those that were too heavily damaged by the bomb attack to survive. Reestablish transportation links, if they are out of commission.

Scenario 4

Bern, Switzerland 1965—Traffic

Difficulty: Easy

Time Limit: 10 Years

Win Condition: Low Average Traffic Density

Complication: Traffic Atherosclerosis

In the Bern scenario, you are plagued with severe traffic jams on your roads and a large negative cash flow draining your treasury. The city of Bern is poorly designed in this scenario, with a lack of public rail transportation and an inefficient use of roads encircling every zone. A zone or building, it should be recalled, needs only one tile touching a road in order to have complete transportation access. The many road intersections, bridges, curving roads, and needless duplication of road coverage for the city's zones and buildings contribute to a state of traffic gridlock. Your mission, should you decide to accept it, is to revamp Bern's antiquated and troublesome road network, and supplement it with a modern and speedy light rail network.

To better appreciate Bern's financial problems, take a look at the Budget window for the 1966 fiscal year. In this budget you should immediately notice your negative cash flow of $–1,876 (your cash flow may differ slightly due to changes you made in your city's infrastructure the previous year). If you don't act to stem the flow of red ink, your coffers will run dry before you have a chance to remake Bern into a commuter's paradise. What could be causing this extraordinary loss? Examining your budget outlays, you will notice that you are spending $2,400 a year for the Police Department, $1,600 a year for the Fire Department, and $1,903 for the Transportation Department. At this point, you should be alarmed at the high costs of maintaining your Police and Fire departments. For a population of only 95,000 people, it is unreasonable to support 24 police stations and 16 fire stations, at a yearly cost of $100 per station. In the strategy section of this step, we will explore ways to trim your budget without adversely affecting Bern.

Strategy

The Bern scenario is the first scenario to use a criterion other than population to judge your actions. To win this scenario you must achieve low average traffic densities within 10 years. The density levels are calculated in your Traffic Density map, and by using this map frequently, you can gauge your progress in reducing traffic problems.

Since you have plenty of time to map out your plans, you shouldn't need to pause the simulator in this scenario. Your strategy will consist of two central elements: first, clear unnecessary roads and replace principal roads with rails; second, reduce the number of police stations and totally eliminate all fire stations.

Of course, clearing and replacing your roads doesn't mean you should immediately rush out with your bulldozer and start hacking away all your roads. Doing so would be a mistake, because you cannot afford to replace all your roads with more expensive rails. You must shrewdly prune your road network of unnecessary branches, and replace with rails only those roads that are heavily travelled. After you have completed this task, you will want to start reducing the excessive number of police and fire stations. Before doing this, you should disable disasters so that you will not have any fire outbreaks when you cut back fire protection services.

By referring to the Traffic Density map, determine where the worst traffic problems are, and remedy them by replacing the road or bridge in question with rail. Traffic conditions change, so from time to time you should glance at this important map to make sure you haven't overlooked any new traffic snarls.

Bulldoze Roads Leading out of the City If you look at your road network, you will see many roads in the southern and northern out-skirts that don't serve any zones or buildings. These "country lanes" are a total waste of money and should be bulldozed immediately.

Build Rail Lines into Downtown Districts There are two methods of dealing with Bern's traffic crisis. The first has you checking the

Traffic Density map for heavy traffic, and then replacing the clogged road(s) with rails. The second method requires you to replace all roads with rails in a way that doesn't require complete tile-for-tile substitution. The next section elaborates on these two techniques.

The first technique is really one of feedback and response. You get feedback from the simulator on traffic patterns, and you respond by building rails to replace the problem roads. Usually traffic bottlenecks will occur in downtown Bern, especially near bridge approaches. If you note the number of intersections that are to be found in Bern, you will quickly understand why this city has a problem with traffic. To alleviate the worst problem spots, bulldoze all but the very northernmost bridge. Replace these bridges and their approach roads with rail tunnels and you will have completed an important step in solving Bern's traffic woes. Next, examine the Traffic Density map to ascertain where the worst traffic snafus are occurring. Once you have pinpointed the arterials that have high traffic, bulldoze them clear and replace with rails. Remember to restore any power lines you knock down so that your zones remain powered. Repeat the process of feedback and response, bulldozing as necessary and replacing with rail to reduce traffic.

The second technique for dealing with traffic involves redesigning the transportation network. The Traffic Density map shows a pretty dismal traffic design situation for Bern. Note how each zone is completely wrapped with road tiles. As noted earlier, this is wasteful and unnecessary, and it creates many more traffic-slowing intersections. More importantly, how do we fix this fundamental design flaw without totally bulldozing the city down? The answer is elegant and simple. What you need to do is bulldoze all the roads in the central downtown areas, and create a serpentine rail line that runs between every other row of zones. Every other row of zones will have a blank space between them, but this doesn't matter since every zone will still touch a rail tile. Figure 17.1 illustrates this concept for a small area of downtown Bern.

As mentioned before, you shouldn't attempt to replace every road tile with rail. This is too expensive a proposition, and is unnecessarily extravagant. Just replace roads that are in busy downtown

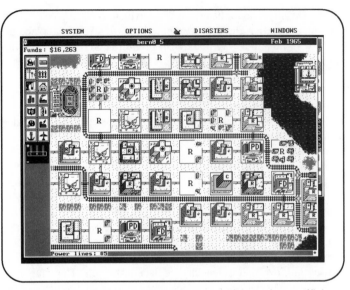

Figure 17.1: Redesigning transportation access for maximum efficiency

districts. You should still plan to bulldoze your bridges and replace them with rail tunnels, since these water crossings tend to be heavily travelled.

 If a drawbridge is up, you will be unable to bulldoze it. Wait till the drawbridge portion has been lowered to regain the ability to bull-doze it away.

Disable Disasters   To prevent any fires or other disasters from foiling your plans, disable disasters. After doing this, you can breathe a little easier when bulldozing churches and fire stations.

Control Negative Cash Flow   As mentioned previously, Bern is awash in a budgetary sea of red ink. Your expenditures for police and fire services will ruin you if you don't act to reduce expenses. You may wonder how to cut back services without adversely affect-ing Bern's crime and fire rates. The solution to this question is simple for the Fire Department. Once you disable disasters, you can cut the Fire Department budget to zero and safely bulldoze all your fire stations without fear of new fires cropping up. This will save you $1,600 a year in maintenance fees. As for the Police Department, police stations can be eliminated if there are other stations nearby that can take up the slack. If you examine your Police Protection map, you can see the areas that have excessively high levels of police protection, and start selectively eliminating stations that are redundant. The 24 police stations you initially start out with can be safely cut back to 14 stations without seriously compromising your crime fighting efforts. Just be sure to occasionally check your Crime Rate map to see if crime has skyrocketed in a particular quarter of your city. The savings from liquidating 10 police stations will net you an additional $1,000 a year to your budget. The combined savings from both the police and fire station cutbacks will be $2,600 a year, more than enough to put your cash flow back into the black.

Bulldoze Selected Zones In some cases you will need to bulldoze zones or buildings to make way for improved transit access to important water crossings or other transportation corridors. Don't be afraid to do this out of fear of losing residents. The win condition for this scenario does not depend on how large your population is. In fact, as discussed below, you can win with zero population.

Alternative Strategy: Destroy Bern

Although it may seem nihilistic to do so, you can win the Bern scenario by destroying the city. Simply bulldoze all zones and buildings and you will eliminate all traffic. If you then wait until the required 10 years have elapsed, you will have won the game by satisfying the win condition of low average traffic density!

Scenario 5

Tokyo, Japan 1957—Monster Attack

Difficulty: Easy

Time Limit: 5 Years

Win Condition: City Score above 500

Complication: Monster Dining on Your City

The Tokyo monster scenario unleashes a Godzilla-like creature on the city of Tokyo, smashing buildings into rubble and touching off fires and explosions. Like the monster that is selected from the Disasters menu, the Tokyo monster is attracted to high levels of pollution and will often head straight for heavy industry, power plants, airports and sea ports. The monster cannot be stopped, but the damage it wreaks can be minimized by scurrying after it and cleaning up the mess it leaves behind. You must put out the fires it starts, repair the utility lines and transportation links it breaks, and undo the damage it causes when trains, ships, helicopters and planes crash.

Although the SimCity documentation claims that the Tokyo monster scenario is "moderately difficult," don't worry—sometimes it is a cinch to beat. In fact this scenario is frequently so easy that you can probably win by doing nothing at all. Occasionally, however, this scenario will present some small challenges which require swift responses. Your success at winning the game really hinges on where the monster first appears in the city. You can't really predict where he will make his stage entrance, but typically he starts out in the waters off of Tokyo harbor and moves in towards the city. For inexplicable reasons, the monster will sometimes wander about aimlessly in the water and never touch land. In such instances all you need to do is sit tight and wait until the required five years have elapsed in order to win the game. On the other hand, if the monster starts wrecking your city and setting off fires and explosions, your score will drop and you will have a tough time restoring your score in time to win.

Strategy

One of the first things you should notice is the shortage of fire stations for a city of Tokyo's size. There are only four fire stations for the entire city. You should build many more fire stations in preparation for the monster attack. This way, when the monster does make his appearance you should have ample firefighting capabilities should fires break out. After completing this task, you will want to follow along behind the monster, attempting to rebuild the infrastructure it destroys as it crawls along. Rubble should be cleared, power lines restored, and fires put out if you are to succeed and win.

Build New Fire Stations   As noted before, four fire stations provide inadequate coverage for the entire city of Tokyo. If you check your Fire Protection map, you will see that the southern part of Tokyo has no fire coverage whatsoever, which is an intolerable situation. Therefore, build five or six more fire stations to thoroughly cover the city. The best locations to situate your new fire stations are on the land occupied by churches and hospitals. If you can't find a decent church or hospital to raze, you must bulldoze an industrial or commercial zone and replace it with a fire station. Remember to first turn off disasters from the Disasters menu before bulldozing churches.

Clean Up Monster Mess   The monster leaves a trail of destruction wherever it goes. Because it knocks down power lines, whole sections of Tokyo may be left without power. Prolonged power loss to the city can cause growth to stop and your city score to decline, so you must respond quickly to power outages. Roads and rails will also be cut, interrupting transportation access to other parts of the city. Try to rebuild these vital links as soon as the monster destroys them, for doing so will allow your city to function despite the carnage that is taking place.

Contain Fires   Undoubtedly you will be faced with fires and explosions if the monster has enough time to thrash around Tokyo. You must respond to these emergencies as you would any other fire—that is, isolate the fires from other combustibles, and make sure that there are fully functioning fire stations nearby.

Reroute Traffic and Rezone If you have time left over to improve your score, you might consider redesigning Tokyo's inefficient and traffic clogged transportation network. This will reduce traffic complaints and make Tokyo a more attractive place to live. Like the city of Bern, Tokyo is laid out in a clumsy "block" design with roads encircling every zone. If you bulldoze the roads and replace them only where needed with rails, you will eliminate the traffic problems and reduce pollution in one fell stroke. Realign zones that get in the way of your plans by bulldozing and replacing as necessary.

High Pollution Levels Harm Your Score High pollution levels, which negatively affect your score, should prompt you to relocate industrial zones further away from residential zones. When doing this, notice that the industrial zones are placed along the waterfront, thereby ruining the potential benefit of high land values due to the proximity of water. It might be a good idea to start replacing industry along the waterfront with commercial and residential zones, and move the industrial zones to the perimeter or outskirts of Tokyo where they can cause little complaint. In the Pollution Index map (Figure 18.1), notice much of the high pollution is along the waterfront, which is a result of the high concentration of industrial zones.

Alternative Strategy: Destroy Tokyo

Because the win condition for this scenario is dependent on your city score being higher than 500, and not upon population size, you can win the Tokyo scenario by completely destroying Tokyo. Bulldoze clear all the buildings to get rid of the residents. Your score will stay above 500 as long as there are no people to grumble, complain and criticize. SimCity residents, you must remember, love to moan and groan about how miserable the conditions are in the city. Unfortunately, the more snivelling they do, the lower your city score. If there are no people, there can be no complaints, and your city score will remain high.

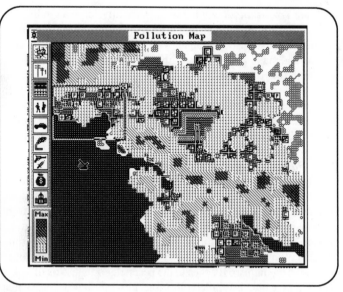

Figure 18.1: Much of the worst pollution is along the waterfront

Scenario 6

Detroit, MI 1972—Crime

Difficulty: Extremely Difficult

Time Limit: 10 Years

Win Condition: Low Average Crime Density

Complication: High Crime

The decline and fall of Detroit is the subject of this scenario. Because of strong foreign competition in automobile manufacturing during the 1970s, Detroit suffered severe recessions, which undermined the local economy and forced large layoffs. The coup de grace, however, was the Arab oil embargo of 1973. With oil prices high, the demand for smaller, fuel-efficient autos forced Detroit to switch from manufacturing large gas-guzzling behemoths to making smaller and thriftier compact cars.

Unfortunately, smaller profit margins on the smaller cars and competition from abroad hurt Detroit's economy and as a result, unemployment rose and property values dropped. Along with these two setbacks, crime began to skyrocket to stratospheric levels, in part due to the faltering economy. In the Detroit scenario, you are expected to rein in the burgeoning crime problem, and revitalize the decaying inner city.

Strategy

Since your primary goal is to lower crime rates, you must start increasing the number of police stations. Before doing this, toggle off disasters in order to eliminate random disasters that might set your plans back. In densely built-up areas, when deciding where to place new police stations, first choose hospitals, churches, and fire stations before bulldozing any other zone type. Because you have limited funds, you will also need to deal with the city's negative cash flow. Since the Transportation Department consumes the lion's share of your budget outlays, you must start bulldozing unnecessary roads and rails. If necessary, cut all transportation funding to bring your cash flow back into the black. After paring your transportation costs, you should turn your attention to the Fire Department and cut all funding. With disasters disabled, you will have no fear of fires erupting in your city. Once you have stabilized the city's cash flow, you can devote more time to improving the "livability" of the city by establishing more parks in industrial areas, and relocating residential and industrial zones so that there is more separation between them. Periodically check your Crime Rate map to reassure yourself that you have dealt the criminals a fatal blow. In 10 years, with low crime rates you should win the scenario and be awarded the key to the city.

Turn Off Disasters Toggle off disasters as your first act of office. This will enable you to focus on your primary problems in Detroit. Why complicate matters further by having to deal with tornados or fires?

Build More Police Stations Looking at the Crime Rate map in the Maps window when you first start the scenario (Figure 19.1), it's not surprising that the heaviest crime, as viewed using the density key, is in the most industrialized sectors of the city.

With these crime rates in mind, you must decide where to place new police stations. You will want to space the stations far enough apart that they won't overlap coverage areas but, at the same time, close enough that they fill in any voids where there is no police protection. At the outset of the game there are only three police stations, whose inadequate coverage leaves vast tracts of city land unprotected.

Build your stations over empty land, when possible, but if this cannot be done, bulldoze hospitals, churches, and fire stations before clearing a residential, commercial, or industrial zone. If you must wipe out one of the latter three zone types, go for empty zones rather than zones with buildings in them.

After constructing your new police stations, make sure that they have power and transportation. Then, call up the Police Protection map to see how much your police presence has increased. To be absolutely satisfied, next turn to the Crime Rate map to see if you

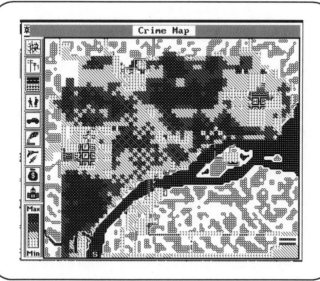

Figure 19.1: The Crime Rate map at the start of the Detroit scenario

have lowered crime in the area. You must check the Crime Rate map throughout the game to make sure that crime does not crop up somewhere else in the city.

Cut Fire Department Funding If you look at the Budget window, you will see that Detroit is experiencing a severe cash crunch. There is a negative cash flow due to excessive spending on the Fire Department. You must turn this bleak situation around, and get Detroit's cash flow back into the black.

To save money, call up the Budget window and reduce Fire Department spending to 0 percent. Since you should have already toggled disasters off, you don't need to maintain your fire stations anymore.

Bulldoze Unneeded Rails and Roads Detroit has many roads and rails that lead out of the city and have no purpose. They serve no zones and carry no traffic, but still cost you in yearly maintenance. Get rid of them.

The transportation network is mostly comprised of roads laid out in a grid pattern. As with Bern, this is terribly inefficient due to useless road redundancy, with each zone having more road access than it needs. Each zone or building requires but one tile with road or rail access to completely satisfy its transportation needs. The additional roads actually generate more traffic, which contributes pollution to the city, causing land values to drop and crime to escalate. If you redesign the city, along the lines of Bern, with rails replacing roads in an alternating row pattern (see Scenario 4), you can do much to alleviate traffic and pollution problems.

Cut Transportation Department Funding If Necessary   Your main concern should be to reduce Transportation Department spending on road and rail maintenance. Do whatever it takes, including cutting funding to 0 percent, if necessary, to bring your cash flow back into the black.

Bulldoze Slums and Replace with Parks   Using the Query function, check the land values for residential zones that are in the inner city. If they are consistently low, this means that the zones are faltering and in need of help. Rather than spending time and money trying to renovate these slums into decent housing, bulldoze the zones and replace with parks.

Zone New Suburbs   To replace the housing that was bulldozed in the previous section, you should establish new suburban residential zones away from the industrial quarter of the city. This way, the displaced Sims from the bulldozed zones can move into the newly fabricated suburbs rather than leave Detroit entirely. Your tax base will increase with the higher suburban land values, and the quality of life, as measured by complaints and your city score, will improve.

Alternative Strategy: Reaganomics

An alternative strategy, more radical and brutish, works in a manner reminiscent of the policy known as Reaganomics. In this strategy, you slash all funding for the Transportation Department and then build police stations galore, sparing no expense to completely and thoroughly flood the city with police. Next, you turn a deaf ear to citizen complaints, and ignore the popularity polls. All you are concerned about is lowering crime, and as the old Machiavellian saying goes, "The ends justify the means." Therefore you need not concern yourself with anything other than crime reduction and balancing your budget.

Build Police Stations   Completely pepper Detroit with police stations. Use the Police Protection map and the Crime Rate map to figure out whether you need more stations in specific areas of the city.

Cut All Transportation and Fire Department Spending   Before slashing spending for the Transportation and Fire departments, toggle off disasters. This will ensure that no fires break out when you cut the Fire Department allocations to 0 percent. Reduce Transportation funding to 0 percent to further maximize your savings. The Sims may not be able to travel and will complain, but you can safely ignore them. You are not too concerned if you lose population.

Ignore Citizen Complaints   Citizens will complain about your policies, but you needn't worry. They cannot impeach you and you are safe from the threat of recall. You can do as you please, because your only care is whether crime is reduced to a negligible level in 10 years time.

Dead City Strategy

If you destroy Detroit by bulldozing all the zones and all the inhabitants leave, you will win the scenario. With no people, there can be no crime and no complaints. Hence, after 10 years have elapsed, you will win because you will have met the win condition of low average crime density.

Scenario 7

Boston, MA 2010—Nuclear Meltdown

Difficulty: Easy

Time Limit: 5 Years

Win Condition: City Score above 500

Complication: Radiation Contamination, Fires, and High Crime

In the Boston scenario, you are faced with the dire consequences of nuclear power gone amuck. One of Boston's nuclear power plants will melt down, igniting fires and leaving the surrounding land poisoned and unusable. At the beginning of the scenario, Boston is already in trouble with high crime and deficit spending plaguing the city. When you step in to take charge, you must battle an already low city score, high disapproval ratings for your predecessor's bungling performance, and vocal citizen complaints about crime and high taxes.

Boston starts out with three nuclear and two coal power plants. In addition, there are only three fire stations and four police stations for all of Boston. Obviously the fire and police protection is inadequate for a city of this size facing a catastrophic disaster. Further compounding your problems, Boston is also experiencing a negative cash flow, which will inhibit any plans you have to improve the situation. Too much money is being spent maintaining an inefficient road network that unnecessarily duplicates road access to zones and buildings. Boston's initial low city score is a reflection of the serious problems of crime, pollution, and general citizen disgruntlement over City Hall's inability to take action.

Strategy

The strategy to beat the Boston scenario is easy. Start by building new fire stations to help control fires around the nuclear power plant located in the lower middle section of Boston. This is the power plant that always melts down. Next, bulldoze fire breaks around the

fires to snuff them out quickly. Perform damage control by bulldozing rubble so that zones and buildings can rebuild. To replace the
power lost by the nuclear power plant, you must build a coal plant
on the east side of Boston. Your main concern after doing this is to
restore power and put an end to the rampant crime that infests the
city. You must build police stations to supplement the meager police
force you start out with, and keep track of the Crime Rate map to
ascertain whether your war on crime is working. Check the Evaluation
window frequently to determine how fast your city score is rising.
Remember that you have only five years to bring the score above
500. With crime reduced to tolerable levels, your city score should
soar, and you will win the scenario.

Build Fire Stations around the Nuclear Power Plant   When you
first start the Boston scenario, you will have only moments before
the meltdown occurs. You already know that there are not enough
fire stations to deal with this emergency, so you should take this
precious time to build a new fire station in the vicinity of the nuclear
power plant located in the south central portion of the city. Doing
this before the accident occurs will help speed the day when the fires
are finally doused.

Build one or two additional fire stations in the area to supplement
the coverage of the first, and you will be certain to quickly extinguish the fires. Make sure that there is power and road access for
each fire station to ensure maximum prophylactic effect.

Avoid Building Next to Radioactive Tiles   When the accident
finally does occur, you will notice radioactive symbols scarring the
land and pockmarking zones and buildings in the area. These
contaminated tiles emit high levels of radiation and are considered
as pollution sources in SimCity. Any zones that contain or are
adjacent to these tiles should be bulldozed. You should also avoid
building any new zones near the contaminated areas, due to their
harmful effect on zone populations and land values. The irradiated
land is useless for the rest of the game, so you might as well cut your
losses and relocate homes and businesses to safer ground.

Bulldoze Fire Breaks   Even though you have built fire stations to
battle the blazes set off by the meltdown, you can help put out the

fires by bulldozing fire breaks around the fires. As discussed earlier in the book, bulldoze all roads, rails, power lines, parks, forests, zones and buildings that border any tile that is on fire. This way the fire cannot spread.

Bulldoze Rubble To effect repairs on uncontaminated zones, or buildings that are slightly damaged, bulldoze any rubble inside them. Provided there is power and transportation access, the zones or buildings can then regenerate the damaged interior portions, thereby restoring full functionality. Roads, rails and utility lines must be rebuilt manually, since they have no self-healing powers.

Build a New Coal Power Plant Your two remaining nuclear and two coal power plants have enough capacity to support your present city. But if you decide to build any new zones or buildings, you will need an additional power plant. Plan now to build a new coal power plant on the outskirts of Boston, where its polluting effects can be minimized.

Restore Power If you notice that there are zones or buildings without power, repair the utility links so that decay doesn't begin to set in.

Build Police Stations Your next major problem, after the fires, is to deal with Boston's high crime problem. The four police stations you start out with cannot begin to deal with the crime problems of a city like Boston. As a consequence, you must build new police stations to thoroughly cover the city and put a damper on crime activities. Use the Crime Rate map in conjunction with the Police Protection map to plot the ideal placement of police stations. If you pinpoint those areas with the highest crime first, you can target the police stations for maximum crime-busting effect. Once you have reduced crime to minimal levels, your city score and population will zoom higher.

Relocate Contaminated Zones to Safer Ground If you have time left over within your allotted five years, you can start "relocating" contaminated zones to safer neighborhoods. Bulldoze down the older zones as you establish new zones, so that you won't inadvertently create shortages of building space for your residents.

Time Permitting, Redesign Inefficient Road Network   Because the Boston scenario is only five years long, you may not have enough time to address the serious budget problems that Boston faces. There is a negative cash flow, due to the high expense of maintaining a huge road network. Most of these roads are unnecessarily redundant, because they encircle zones and provide more zone contact than is needed. A more efficient transportation design might use the ideas presented in the Bern scenario, where roads were bulldozed and replaced with alternating rows of rail lines (see Scenario 4).

Scenario 8

Rio de Janeiro, Brazil 2047—Flood

Difficulty: Easy

Time Limit: 10 Years

Win Condition: City Score above 500

Complication: Flooding

The greenhouse's effect on the ecosystems of the Earth is the subject of the Rio de Janeiro scenario. In this scenario, the atmospheric gases emitted by industries have caused the Earth to warm by 4 degrees Fahrenheit in the mid-21st century. As a consequence of this warming, the polar ice caps melt and sea levels rise. Rio de Janeiro is especially susceptible to flood damage due to the low elevation of the land, and also because of the high number of dwellings that are in close proximity to the water.

Looking at some of the initial statistics for Rio, you should note that your beginning city score is blissfully high with a score of over 780. Since the outcome of this scenario is dependent on your final city score, this will come as good news to you. For a city that is suffering from the consequences of global warming, however, it is ironic to note that Rio is powered by no fewer than nine coal power plants. The carbon dioxide emissions from this type of plant are strongly implicated in creating the greenhouse effect. There are no nuclear power plants to lessen the burden on the atmosphere.

Strategy

This strategy makes use of the simulator's ability to vary speeds. You will want to keep the game speed slow so that you may take your time reacting to the flooding disasters. If you need more time, you can always use the **Pause** feature to freeze the simulator while you zone or build. Before going on, though, disable disasters so that you can avoid random disasters messing up your game.

A few moments after the scenario starts, you will get reports of flooding. At this point, you should take note of the location(s) of the flooding, using the Maps window to plot its precise position. The flooding occurs in certain areas of the city more than others; by keeping track, you can remember not to use the affected land again in the same way. As zoning czar, you will want to avoid rebuilding on flood-prone lands.

Since there is a persistent brownout problem, your next order of business is to build a new power plant. A nuclear power plant will serve your needs best, since it can provide power for approximately 150 zones and buildings. Next, examine the crime problem using the Crime Rate map. High crime should be dealt with by building new police stations in the areas concerned.

Flooded zones and buildings should be bulldozed clear and replaced with parks. Parks will increase land values, and if they are flooded again, will not cause you the grief that occupied zones would. The bulldozed zones should be replaced by zoning new housing and businesses on higher ground farther inland. There is plenty of land available for this purpose in the western portion of the city, with its densely forested terrain.

Keep the Game Speed Slow The Rio scenario, by default, starts out at the Slow speed setting. This speed should be adhered to so that you have ample time to execute your plans. If you need extra time, select **Pause**.

Disable Disasters Do yourself a favor. Disable disasters for less frustration. There is nothing worse than nearly winning a scenario only to have your city ruined, at the last instant, by an earthquake.

Build a New Power Plant Rio does not have enough power generation capacity to provide for all its zones and buildings. Build a nuclear power plant, preferably far away from the shoreline.

Track Crime and Build More Police Stations Using the Crime Rate map, track the areas with the worst crime. Place new police stations in these neighborhoods to reduce crime to tolerable levels.

If you have difficulty deciding where to establish the stations, first demolish churches, hospitals, and fire stations before clearing any other zone type. Periodically check the Crime Rate map to make sure that crime hasn't shifted to some other part of the city.

Keep Track of Where Flooding Occurs   By observing where flooding is occurring, you can alter land use policies so that homes and businesses are prohibited in these areas. Even though the flood waters may recede, leaving empty land, you cannot be sure that flooding will not happen again in the future. By restricting the land use to parks or empty space, you can avoid the problems of future flood disasters.

Bulldoze Flooded Zones and Buildings   Clear away flood damaged zones and buildings completely. You will want to avoid a future repetition of this kind of damage. It is futile to rebuild on the same land; you will only be rewarded with more flooding.

Replace Flooded Zones with Parks   Building parks in formerly flooded zones will help raise land values for nearby properties and will buffer you against future flood damage. Unlike flooded zones, parks that are flooded have no discernable impact on your economy, so losing them to floods is not a big deal.

Relocate Flooded Zones to Higher Ground   You must "relocate" to safer ground the inundated zones that you bulldozed earlier. This step is necessary so that you don't lose population and harm your city score. An ideal location for new zones is the forested section of western Rio. Build roads, power lines, and police stations in this new section of the city so that growth can proceed uninterrupted.

Appendix A

SimCity File Format Description

This appendix describes the city data file format for SimCity. If you have any interest in customizing your city by directly modifying the city file, the information below will help you find the data structures you need to change. This description is valid for both the IBM and Macintosh versions of SimCity. On the PC, you can edit the file (PC city files have the extension .CTY) using disk editing utilities such as Norton Utility's DiskEdit, or PC Tools. Norton Utilities for the Macintosh will allow you to edit the Macintosh city files. The list below identifies the principal data structures in the order they appear within the city file:

FinderInfo: Although this part of the file is only used by the Macintosh, the IBM versions also create this in every file so that cities can be easily moved to the Mac. *480 bytes*

ResHis: This is the data represented by the Residential Population graph seen in the Graphs window. The first 120 integers represent the 10-year data (most recent first) and the second 120 integers represent the 120-year data. *480 bytes*

ComHis: This is the data represented by the Commercial Population graph seen in the Graphs window. The first 120 integers represent the 10-year data (most recent first) and the second 120 integers represent the 120-year data. *480 bytes*

IndHis: This is the data represented by the Industrial Population graph seen in the Graphs window. The first 120 integers represent the 10-year data (most recent first) and the second 120 integers represent the 120-year data. *480 bytes*

CrimeHis: This is the data represented by the Crime Level graph seen in the Graphs window. The first 120 integers represent the 10-year data (most recent first) and the second 120 integers represent the 120-year data. The data is scaled between 0 and 255. *480 bytes*

PolluteHis: This is the data represented by the Pollution Level graph seen in the Graphs window. The first 120 integers represent the 10-year data (most recent first) and the second 120 integers represent the 120-year data. (Scaled from 0 to 255.) *480 bytes*

CashFlowHis: This is the data represented by the CashFlow graph seen in the Graphs window. The first 120 integers represent the 10-year data (most recent first) and the second 120 integers represent the 120-year data. (Scaled 0 to 255, with 128 as the midpoint: values smaller than 128 indicate negative cash flow, values larger than 128 indicate positive cash flow.) *240 bytes*

MiscVar: This is an array of integers (*24,000 bytes total*) used to store the following items:

MiscVar[1]	External Market Size
MiscVar[2]	Residential Population
MiscVar[3]	Commercial Population
MiscVar[4]	Industrial Population
MiscVar[5]	Residential Value
MiscVar[6]	Commercial Value
MiscVar[7]	Industrial Value
MiscVar[8&9]	City Time (current year=City Time/48 +1900)
MiscVar[10]	CrimeRamp (used to smooth graphs)
MiscVar[11]	PolluteRamp (used to smooth graphs)
MiscVar[12]	LandValue Average
MiscVar[13]	Crime Average
MiscVar[14]	Pollution Average
MiscVar[15]	Game Level
MiscVar[16]	City Class (village, town, city, etc.)
MiscVar[17]	City Score

MiscVar[50&51]	Total Funds (long value)
MiscVar[52]	Flag for Auto-Bulldozer
MiscVar[53]	Flag for Auto-Budget
MiscVar[54]	Flag for Auto-Goto
MiscVar[55]	Flag for Sound On/Off
MiscVar[56]	City Tax Rate
MiscVar[57]	Simulation Speed
MiscVar[58&59]	Police Budget
MiscVar[60&61]	Fire Budget
MiscVar[62&63]	Road Budget

Map: This is the city map. The map is made up of 120 horizontal by 100 vertical tiles (*27,248 bytes total*). Each tile is represented by a 16-bit integer: bits 0 through 9, the Tile Index, identify the type of tile, and bits 10 through 15 identify the "attributes" for that tile. The following list shows the Tile Index categories arranged by decimal value:

Value of Bits 0–9	*Tile Index Category*
0	Clear Terrain
2	All Water
4	River Channel
5–20	River Edges
21–36	Tree Edges
37	All Trees
40–43	Parks
44–47	Rubble
48–51	Flood
52	Radiation
56–63	Fire

64–78	Roads (no traffic)
80–142	Roads (light traffic)
144–206	Roads (heavy traffic)
208–222	Power Lines
224–238	Transit Lines
244	Low-Density and Empty Residential Zone Center
249–260	Houses
265, 274, 283, 292	Residential Zone Centers (low value), from Low to High Density
301, 310, 319, 328	Residential Zone Centers (mid value)
337, 346, 355, 364	Residential Zone Centers (upper value)
373, 382, 391, 400	Residential Zone Centers (high value)
409	Hospital Center Tile
418	Church center tile
427	Commercial empty zone center
436, 445, 454, 463, 472	Commercial zone centers (low value) 436 lowest density
481, 490, 499, 508, 517	Commercial zone centers (mid value)
526, 535, 544, 553, 562	Commercial zone centers (upper value)
571, 580, 589, 598, 607	Commercial zone centers (high value)
616	Industrial empty zone center
625, 634, 643, 652	Industrial zone centers (low value)

661, 670, 679, 688	Industrial zone centers (high value)
698	Port Center Tile
716	Airport Center Tile
750	Coal Power Plant Center Tile
765	Fire Station Center Tile
774	Police Station Center Tile
784	Stadium (empty) Center Tile
800	Stadium (full) Center Tile
816	Nuclear Power Plant Center Tile
828–831	Open Horizontal Bridge
832–839	Radar Dish
840–843	Park Fountain
948–951	Open Vertical Bridge

The following list shows the tile attributes indicated by bits 10 through 15.

Bit Number	Tile Attribute
Bit[10]	Is this a zone center tile?
Bit[11]	Is this tile animated?
Bit[12]	Is this tile bulldozable?
Bit[13]	Can this tile burn?
Bit[14]	Can this tile conduct power?
Bit[15]	Is this tile currently powered?

Appendix B

Using the SimCity Terrain Editor

With the SimCity Terrain Editor, an add-on software package from Maxis, you can sculpt landscape features to suit your tastes. Rather than being dependent on randomly generated terrain, you can place trees, open land, lakes, rivers, and oceans anywhere on your city map. In addition, you can change the date, name, and play level of your cities, and design new shipping routes for your ships. When you are finished, you can load your newly designed terrain into SimCity or any of the *Graphics Sets* (see Appendix C for a description of Graphics Sets). You can also import a previously created city, alter its landscape features or any man-made objects, and then return to play the city with its newly sculpted geography. In Step 13 you saw the Terrain Editor trick of reducing your airport and sea port to a smaller size, thus limiting pollution to a smaller area. Using the Terrain Editor, you can design a highly compact city, like the Mill2 city you saw in Step 13, by squeezing more zones into your land space.

Using the Terrain Editor

You must install the Terrain Editor using the special install program that comes on the Terrain Editor diskette(s). The program is available on two 5¼" 360K disks, or one 3½" disk. A menu of choices will allow you to customize your installation for your particular hardware setup.

You operate the Terrain Editor like you would SimCity; that is, you have windows in which you select icon tools to accomplish particular tasks. There is an Edit window and a Maps window, and you have six icon tools to reshape your landscape. The icon tools allow you to fill in empty land (the *DIRT* icon), place forests (the *TREES* icon), establish new rivers (the *RIVER* icon), set new shipping channels for ships (the *CHANNEL* icon), fill in large areas of the map with trees, water, or empty land (the *FILL* icon), and undo the last operation you performed (the *UNDO* icon).

Unlike SimCity, the Terrain Editor allows you to use your icon tools to build in both the Edit window and the Maps window. However, you must paint very slowly when sculpting terrain in the Maps window, because of the greater amount of land that must be covered by the pointer.

Building a River

To illustrate how one might use the Terrain Editor, lets try building a small river tributary. With the Terrain Editor on screen, select the **RIVER** icon tool and start placing river tiles over some land. Notice that the river appears "blocky" and rough. Later you can smooth out these rough edges so that the river is more pleasing and aesthetic to look at.

Building Some Forests

Next, let's try building some forests. Select the **TREES** icon and start placing trees on some empty land. Again, the appearance of the new element is blocky and ugly to look at, but you can smooth it out later. Figure B.1 shows the appearance of newly sculpted river and forest tiles before and after they have been "smoothed" using the **Smooth Everything** option under the Terrain menu.

Filling Large Areas with Dirt, Trees, or Water

To use the **FILL** icon tool, you must first select either the *DIRT*, *TREES*, or *RIVER* icon, and then outline the area on the map that you wish to fill. You outline by drawing a continuous unbroken line of land, water, or trees to enclose the area you wish filled—without any gaps. You may work in either the Maps or Edit windows. Next, after making sure you have left no gaps in the outline, select the **FILL** icon and then click in the middle of the area you have outlined. The outlined area should fill with the terrain feature that you previously selected. If the fill "bleeds," or "spills" outside of the outlined area, then you must select the **UNDO** icon and start anew.

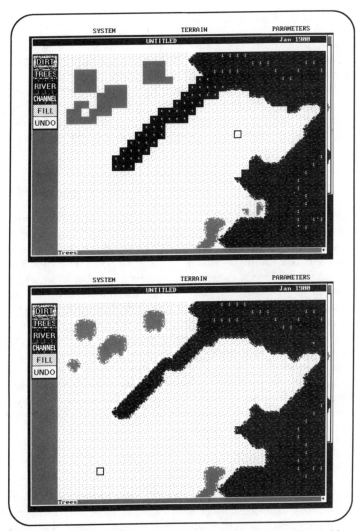

Figure B.1: Sculpting a new river and some forests (top) and smoothing them (bottom)

Plotting the Course of Your Ships

The **CHANNEL** icon tool allows you to specify the path that ships must follow when cruising your waterways. You must place the channel markers in a continuous line. In addition, one end of the channel path must exit off at least one edge of the map. If you place channel tiles too close to land, or even on land, your ships will most likely crash. To erase any misplaced channel tiles, select the **RIVER** icon and click over the channel tile. The channel marker will be replaced by water.

Adjusting Parameters for Random Terrain Generation

You can use the Terrain Editor to automatically generate "randomly" terraformed landscapes while specifying the relative proportions of trees and lakes, and the "curviness" of rivers, by selecting the **Generate Random Terrain** option under the Terrain menu, which brings up the Terrain Creation Parameters dialog box. You set the percentage from 0 to 100 percent using arrow buttons to the left and right of each percentage indicator as seen in Figure B.2. Setting the river curviness to 0 percent will actually prevent any rivers from appearing on your map. Likewise, setting the number of trees and lakes to 0 percent will eliminate any forests or lakes from being generated when the land is terraformed. When you are finished with your selections, click the **Go** button and your new terrain will be generated. Note that the **Start New City** option under the System menu does not use the parameters you set in this dialog box; instead it creates a new, featureless map.

Other Options

Other nifty features of the Terrain Editor include the ability to completely clear the map of all features, or clear only unnatural, constructed objects. You can also create islands. (Islands can only be created using the **Generate Random Terrain** option, and cannot be created using the **Start New City** menu option.)

1. Pull down the Terrain menu and select the **Create Island** option. This menu item is a toggle: that is, it is either on or off. In this case you want to toggle it on.

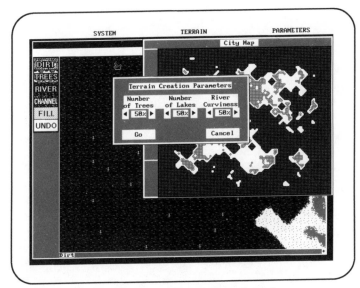

Figure B.2: The Terrain Creation Parameters dialog box

2. Next, select the **Generate Random Terrain** option from
    the Terrain menu. When the dialog box pops up, decide
    whether you want to increase or decrease the number of
    trees and lakes on your island, or adjust the river curviness.
    After completing this, click the **Go** button to have your
    island terraformed.

Appendix C

Using SimCity Graphics Sets 1 & 2

The SimCity Graphics Sets are add-on packages from Maxis that allow you to recreate cities in the past and in the future. When you run any of the Graphics Sets, you will find that the appearance, messages, and sounds of your cities have changed to reflect the character of the historical period you are in. However, the mathematical model that governs SimCity remains unchanged, which means that you will still play SimCity exactly the way you did before. In effect, the changes you see are purely cosmetic: there is no real difference between a city you choose to play in the "Classic Graphics" mode or one that you play in the Medieval Times mode or any other mode. For example, a coal power plant becomes a well, a nuclear power plant becomes a water wheel, a stadium becomes a sumo arena, and rails become rickshaw paths. All the other zone and building types and the disasters also change to something more appropriate for the region or period.

When you play any of the eight original scenarios of SimCity, it will display the same city name and date as the original. But the graphics used on screen will be from the currently selected Graphics Set. For example, if you choose to play the Dullsville scenario in Ancient Asia, your city will open normally with the Dullsville name and date, but will have totally different graphic symbols representing the different zoning and building icons used in designing your city.

Graphics Set #1, which is called Ancient Cities, has three different historical periods in which you can play: Ancient Asia, Medieval Times, and the Wild West. Graphics Set #2, called Future Cities, offers three different future epochs: Future USA, Future Europe, and Moon Colony.

Installing the Graphics Sets

You must install the Graphics Sets using the special install program that comes on the Graphics Sets diskette. The program will modify your version of SimCity, giving it an additional menu option on your System or File menu. The option, called **Load Graphics**, brings up a dialog box in which you can select one of the alternate historical modes of your installed Graphics Sets. Figure C.1 illustrates the dialog box that pops up on screen when you select this command after installing both Graphics Sets 1 and 2.

Ancient Cities

Ancient Asia

Ancient Asia (Figure C.2) is supposed to evoke a mystical mix of ancient Asian cultures. You are Shogun in the year 1234, and you must guide your city from small agrarian villages to great centers of trade and commerce. Along the way, you must deal with disasters from earthquakes, typhoons, tsunamis, and Chinese dragons.

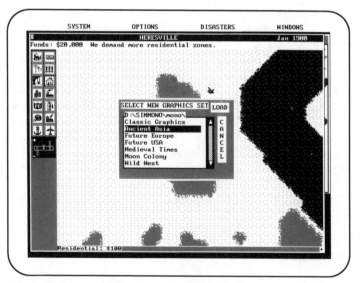

Figure C.1: The Load Graphics dialog box

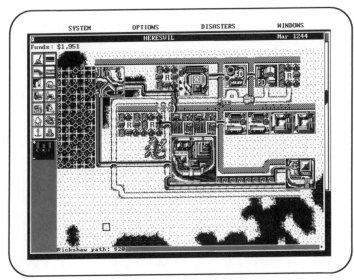

Figure C.2: Ancient Asia

Medieval Times

Medieval Times (Figure C.3) brings back the age of heraldry and chivalry. It is the year 1591, and you are lord master of your fiefdom. Under your magnificent patronage, your serfs will try to build a large kingdom with wind-powered textile mills, aqueduct systems, and castles. Entertainment will be provided in the form of great jousting tournaments. As a nobleman, you must protect your people from the onslaughts of plagues, dragon blasts, and witches.

Wild West

The Wild West (Figure C.4) brings back the excitement and rush of boom times in the American West of the 1800s. As mayor of a frontier town, you must keep the peace, battle range fires, rebuild from the damage caused by twisters, and recover from balloon crashes and poisoned water supplies.

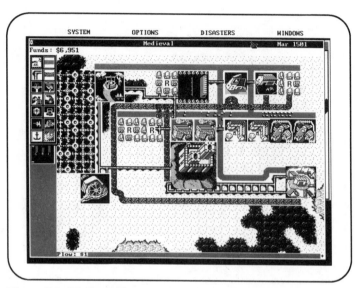

Figure C.3: Medieval Times

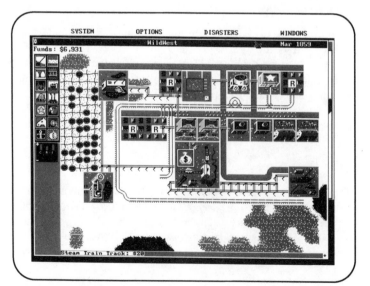

Figure C.4: Wild West

Future Cities

Future USA

Future USA (Figure C.5) is a peek at what America might look like in the 21st century. Your Sims commute in this high-tech future in computer-controlled pods travelling through tubes kept at low air pressure. Magnetic rail trains handle higher-density commuter traffic. When you want to unwind after a hard day, you might consider going to the LaserBot Arena, where robots have replaced humans in a faster and more furiously paced game of football.

Future Europe

Future Europe (Figure C.6) gives you a high-tech glimpse of what Europe might look like in the year 2155. You will still be plagued by the usual assortment of SimCity disasters—earthquakes, floods,

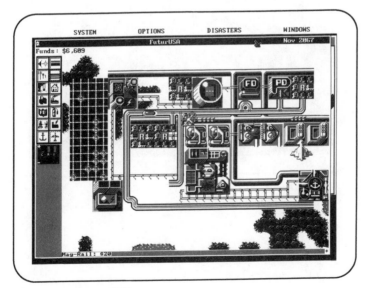

Figure C.5: Future USA

fires, tornados, monsters, and air crashes. A new disaster you will have to guard against is the bio-hazard contamination of land as a result of a bio-lab accident.

Moon Colony

Moon Colony (Figure C.7) offers you a chance to see what life will be like in a colony on the moon. The year is 2195, and you are in charge of mankind's first lunar colony. You must keep an eye out for the new disasters of alien monsters, meteor showers, extraterrestrial viral plagues, and creeping acidic fungus molds.

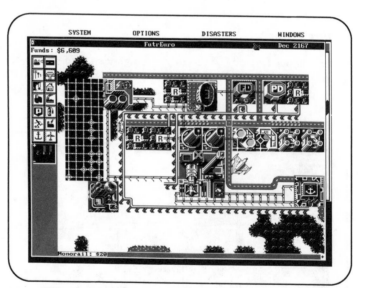

Figure C.6: Future Europe

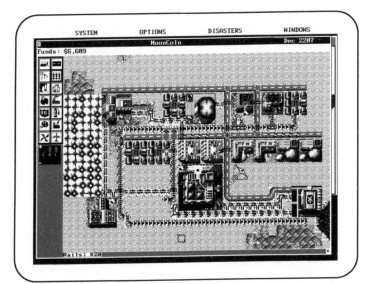

Figure C.7: Moon Colony

Index

Command-Key Combinations for the Mac

⌘-A	Activate Auto-Bulldoze option
⌘-B	Open Budget window
⌘-E	Open Edit window
⌘-G	Open Graphs window
⌘-L	Load City
⌘-M	Open Maps window
⌘-N	Start New City
⌘-Q	Quit SimCity
⌘-S	Save City
⌘-V	Open Evaluation window
⌘-1	Slow speed
⌘-2	Medium speed
⌘-3	High speed
⌘-0	Pause